AFTERGLOW

AFTERGLOW

PAT PARSONS

Copyright © 2022 by Pat Parsons.

All rights reserved. No part of this book may be reproduced in any form or by any electronic or mechanical means, including information storage and retrieval systems, without permission in writing from the publisher, except by reviewers, who may quote brief passages in a review.

ISBN: 978-1-957054-72-8 (Paperback Edition)
ISBN: 978-1-957054-73-5 (Hardcover Edition)
ISBN: 978-1-957054-71-1 (E-book Edition)

Library of Congress Control Number: 2022901509

Book Ordering Information

Phone Number: 315 288-7939 ext. 1000 or 347-901-4920
Email: info@globalsummithouse.com
Global Summit House
www.globalsummithouse.com

Printed in the United States of America

CONTENTS

Chapter 1	"Young Love's Luster"	19
Chapter 2	"Sweet Little Sheila's"	23
Chapter 3	"Separate Ways"	31
Chapter 4	"Grass Skirts Tell Tails"	35
Chapter 5	Cigars And A Southern KUM-fort Shower And My First Shaved Pussy	37
Chapter 6	"Cigars a Southern KUM-fort Shower"	43
Chapter 7	My Ball-Busting/Prune-Bonding Sex Instructor/Student	47
Chapter 8	"Our Rock Creek Parkway"	57
Chapter 9	"Dual Gratification Personified"	65
Chapter 10	"The 2 Student Boogie"	107
Chapter 11	Double duty/Double pleasure	123
Chapter 12	"My Blueberry Donut-Hole Lover"	127
Chapter 13	Fraulein fever	141
Chapter 14	Rapturized Ruby	159
Chapter 15	"Wedding Bells"	185

ABOUT THE AUTHOR

I was born in a small town in southern Virginia near the Tennessee border. I graduated from high school and got a job. I got into trouble several times, mostly from partaking of the forbidden fruits.

Barely managing not to get shot or go to jail, I decided I would be better off in a more densely populated area where everybody did not know everybody else's business. I moved to a larger city where I was able to work on many different projects at the same time without looking over my shoulder in the process. Now my home is right where I belong. Yes, my home and my heart are permanent residents in the same place they spent the majority of their life.

I live with the afterglow of memories, in the mid to lower abdomen area of all the ladies who have worked miracles for me!!! I am extremely happy there. I hope you enjoy filtering through the memories with me and one of my favorite counterparts, **that Infamous Midnight Mumbler.** He lives everywhere, you know!!!

Yours truly, Pat Parsons

<u>Prelude to Introduction</u>
of
<u>AFTERGLOW</u>

<u>by</u>
<u>"The Midnight Mumbler"</u>

Hyperbole, yes hyperbole – is a word, dumb ass
you will find the meaning in the looking glass
if you see yourself and hold your place

the end of an era you might erase
if you choose to look into the deep
it tells not the time of life that's cheap
oh, the lack of luster one must feel
when genius trumps what's really real
when all life's pleasures are at large
is there no excitement to your charge
denial must be, cry me to sleep

if all that's left, is for you to weep
from here to for and nothing more
gives life one option, shut the door!!!
But then, your genius does explode
into a verbiage mother-load

and once again you can proclaim
there is no fire without a flame

that flame that never sets me free
that flame that burns inside of me
the flame that fires my heart and soul
the flame that never lets me go

'tis there, it's there no matter where
once more, to go from here to there
without the question of but where!!!
Who knows where it is all going

do you know what you're doing
if I thought for one minute that I knew
do you think I'd do the things I do
one serves life as a peasant slave
to wish for things they cannot have
watching others that have flourished
feeling motherless, unloved, unnourished
though contradiction fill the air
it may be time I should declare
the one that holds my heart and soul
is the one that truly has control

and I will happily confess
'tis the one that I love best
she sure gave my heart a whirl
she was my world, she was my girl
from then and now to afterlife
she was my wife, she was my wife!!!

****

The Midnight Mumbler never sleeps
his whole existence is to weep
and search for memories that grow
all through his world of _"afterglow"_!!!

****

INTRODUCTION TO AFTERGLOW

THE book, "Afterglow", is a continuation or afterthought if you will, of previous books by the same author. Such as, "The great American Rabbit Chase" and "Split-tales of "Split-tails", along with some others which may have been in triple X poetry book form. Its content is of events that took place in his life from early childhood, through what you might call, borderline adult – to old age.

Although some of the events might seem, to a point, repetitive by description. The taking place of these events with different participants, I believe is portrayed and explained so you can understand they are the type of events that might require some repetitive actions. Which under no circumstances does this suggest the events in this book are less important, appreciated, or attractive than the events in the aforementioned books were. What it does reflect, is how important these events were to the author. This is revealed by the excessive amount of time spent creating an afterglowic atmosphere he needed for whatever event may be taking place at the time. He always strived to create heartfelt mental memories that his partners could never forget, hence the forming of his wonderful world of afterglow.

It would have been impossible to include every event of this nature that took place in the author's life from age 3 to 51 in one book. Therefore, his wonderful world of Afterglow was created, and the infamous Midnight Mumbler was born. The events depicted in this book where from the crying times after midnight in his world of afterglow. They were found somewhere in a cobweb covered corner waiting to be discovered by the Midnight Mumbler, so their story could be told. Although the authors, as he describes it, Wonderful World of Afterglow is a very pleasant and happy place where he enjoys residence. The Midnight Mumbler is blinded to this the happiness. He does, however, find solace in the discovery of hiding places for the meaningful happenings of lovers and their long-lost past. He considers his job well done by bringing these hidden memories from cobweb corner through the ages to these pages with their heartfelt horniness still intact. He has found so many memorable hidden events. There will certainly be more future revealing to take place. And so much more to

KUM!!!
We all hope you will enjoy every one of them!!!

Synopsis
of

AFTERGLOW

The book afterglow is a reflection of the final resting place for many unmeasurable and meaningful memories in the art of making love. All events share equal status, no matter the length or depth. There is not one event holding higher regard or of more importance than another. If it were not so, the art of making love would be lopsided.

The kiss of a tit, the touch of a twat, the popping of a prune, or the licking of a cunt, or with the overwhelming influence of sex we jumped each other's bones and fucked ourselves silly. These events are all a part of the art of making love. Just as much so as the tender touch of my lips caressed the soft overlay of her nipples and I began to spread the inner lips of her vaginal canal with my thumb and forefinger, she suddenly displayed the favorable reception of rear entry, with the kiss massaging of her pussy lips my tongue found her glorious clitoris as we joined forces to complete the effortless task of making love and we became one.

Although the interest of sex was primed by what might have been a verbal slip from one of his aunts in the early stages of the author's life. From what we understand it could also have been somewhat hereditary. The fact is, all through the early stages of his life, women were extremely attentive and treated him very nice. They seemed to always make an effort to show that he was special, and they wanted to please and take care of him.

It is understood he performs the way he does not only because he loves to, but he wants to, it is somewhat of a repayment process. The events that took place with his playmates and babysitter, his nurses and candy stripers, determined his lifestyle. When someone chooses this path of travel, they must understand the best way to spend their later years are with the memories created throughout their life. If one wants to be happy in their little world of afterglow, they must make some very good memories. This author did just that.

There was a several year span in his life, probably 25 or 30 years that he never let the afterglow of memories for lovemaking events leave his mind. He was trained very well by older females whether they be nurses, candy strippers, babysitters or just women he solicited for training purposes. As a result, the number of hidden memories in the cobweb corners of his world of afterglow mounted to some unknown number.

That of course was the sole purpose of his world of afterglow. He created it by taking notes, making tapes, and taking pictures, with his world of afterglow in mind. Through his self-made memoirs, the preservation of so many wonderful memories could be brought to life. He made the decision while he was still quite young that he would write his memoirs when he retired.

He took up residence in his wonderful world of afterglow to once again, through the winter of his life, relive the life he had created while bringing it to literary form for an audience that might enjoy reading about it. I know the authors greatest wish is for everyone to enjoy the rather literarily picturesque portrayal of memories that cover the walls, hide in the corners, fill the closets and dresser drawers, and inhabit his pillows, throughout his **"WONDERFUL WORLD OF AFTERGLOW"!!!.**

May your life be filled with happy memories.

This is a SEX Book

(NOTICE)
Pure and simple sex from the 60s and 70s!!!
Read at your own risk

Chapter 1

"Young Love's Luster"

****

It was 1956 and I was a sophomore in high school. I was walking home from school one Friday afternoon about 4:30 when I heard someone calling my name. I thought I recognized the voice, I turned to see if I was right and sure enough, I was. It was one of my high school playgirls, per'se, named Michelle. She had a sister, actually, a half-sister, her name was Sheila. They were about the same age, and both were sophomores.

Michelle had been trying to get my attention to see if I would like to attend a surprise birthday party the next day for Sheila. I informed her that I would love to come and asked if I would be expected to wear a suit and tie or casual clothes. Michelle replied with, "I am sure it doesn't matter to Sheila. But I believe, much like myself, she would probably prefer to see you naked." I responded to that request by saying, "Why Michelle, do tell, you are a nature's girl. I would never have guessed. You always seem so prim and proper and just oozing with naivety. Maybe we should try to work something out for the three of us. Oh, by the way, is your mother going to be the chaperone? If so, maybe we could make it the four of us." Michelle came back with, "Yes Patrick, mama is going to be there, and you better watch your step. She doesn't trust you and she is going to keep an eye on you, I am sure. Unfortunately for you it is not the kind of eye you wish it were. What in the hell is wrong with you? Where does this thing that you have for my mother come from? Isn't Sheila and myself enough for you?" I said, "My dear darling Michelle, you, and your sweet lovable sexy sister Sheila are so much more than I deserve, and I could never get enough of either of you. So, I am left with an undying desire for a taste of the fire that bore the seeds of hereditary beauty and sensual sexiness that makes you both so overwhelmingly appealing to my senses. Sooner or later, your mother will have me whether she wants me or not." She said, you are damn right she will have you. If you act on your feelings tomorrow, she will have your ass put in jail. We both want you to come but try to behave yourself. I am sure my mother would love to see you also, just don't get stupid." I replied, "Oh no, it's going to be another one of those no fun parties. Well, if you insist, I will be on my best behavior. Tell Sheila and your mother hello." I blew her a kiss and winked and waved goodbye.

So many moments of afterglow were moving memories through my mind. Thinking of Michelle and Sheila and the fun we had molding our relationship into wide-open completeness. For a long, long time there had been nothing either of us could or would try to hide from each other. We were good friends. We were best friends. I perhaps was the luckiest of the three. Being a guy, it is impossible not to be the recipient of certain information unavailable to most when you are best friends with two very pretty young ladies. I was watching and helping them grow as they did me. We managed and monitored through some of the most difficult and important learning years life has to offer. We were totally in tune with each other. They knew all of me and I knew all of them. I remember when they had their first period, and I am absolutely positive, they both can remember when I had my first orgasm. They were both there watching and waiting with as much interest and anticipation as I. Now, here we all are going on 15 and our relationship has never faltered. I do not believe it ever shall. We are so much a part of one another we sometimes all fall asleep in the same bed while napping after school. If the truth were known that probably happens every night even though one or maybe two of us are missing from a dream. Afterglow happens so fast and lasts so long. Afterglow is forever.

I had to make preparations for the party, as far as what I was going to wear and buying a present. I thought to myself, I wonder what Mrs. Sisslor would say if I showed up in a bow tie and a jockstrap. I know she worries about us being so close at our present ages. Especially with the dynamics of growth, fertility and curiosity being so easily projected and interpreted by eye contact as a part of all our lives. I think I will take it easy on her and make my appearance as a clean-cut young man fully clad.

Chapter 2

"Sweet Little Sheila's"

Special Surprise

****

I had to buy Sheila a present and a birthday card for etiquette' sake. Michelle and I had conjured up a very special present for her. I hope Michelle will make sure we have the privacy to properly present it to her. I gave her the same present on her 15th birthday. Michelle was so pleased and happy she could not wait for Sheila to receive the same.

At some point during the party Michelle and I had planned to isolate Sheila from the rest of the party. It was important that we accomplish this to make a proper presentation of Sheila's party pleasures, or present. We knew it would not be the easiest thing we ever had to do, still it must be done.

The party was going very well as normal surprise parties do. Sheila and Michelle's mother were enjoying themselves more than we expected. Since she was the only person at the party old enough to legally consume alcohol, it appeared she was not being bashful about doing so. Mrs. Sisslor was supposed to be the adult in charge, or party chaperone. Instead, by two hours into the party flavor she was beginning to show signs of tipsiness. Although she was a very beautiful lady, I believe she might have been having trouble with the possibilities of her pleasurable party times having passed her by. It seemed like everyone there to Mrs. Sisslor, in one way or another, was a pleasure to visually consume.

The next thing I knew Mrs. Sisslor walked up to me and said, "Patrick, in case you do not know, I am the mother of that very pretty and sweet little Sheila you have been admiring." I jumped in quickly with, "No ma'am, that cannot be possible, you must have misspoken. Are you sure you did not mean to say you were her sister? You cannot possibly be old enough to be her mother, you look almost as young as she is. Although, you do possess a similar generic beauty resemblance." She replied, I am her mother, and my name is Shelley. You are very kind and just as smooth. I have heard lots about you, and I expect you to be as much of a gentleman with my daughter as you have been with me. And I expect you to refer to me as Mrs. Sisslor." I flirtatiously tried to make it seem like an unconscious mistake and said, Shelley, that is a very pretty name Mrs. Sisslor. It kind of has an ear ringing rhythm, very much the same as Sheila. I like that, now I can hear you both at the same time. One in one ear and one in the other. What more could I ask for? How is it I have never had the pleasure of meeting you before? I am as close if not closer than a brother to both Sheila and Michelle." She replied, "Never mind the question just remember to act the part about being as close as a brother."

By the time the party had got into full swing Mrs. Sisslor had seemingly vanished. I think she must be scared of being the adult, or the one in charge, so she decided to give herself and us a break. That is all Michelle and I needed to know to get Sheila's pleasure trip underway. Michelle checked the bathroom and the bedroom while I checked to see if her car was gone. She was not in the bathroom, or the bedroom and her car was still in the garage, where in the hell did she go? We continued our inconspicuous search for Mrs. Sisslor. In the meantime, Sheila had gone to her room to wait for us.

After about a half hour we decided to present Sheila with her gift. As we opened the door to her bedroom Mrs. Sisslor greeted us with, "Come on in we've been expecting you. What took you so long to find us? Tell me Patrick, what kind of present do you have in mind for my Sheila." I really wanted to tell her the truth. In the back of my mind, I was having a dream with visions of grandeur that included her participation. Michelle and I looked at each other and at the same time said, "We were wondering where you were. We have both been looking for you." I continued with, "Mrs.

Sisslor, you really had us worried. We thought you were going to miss getting to see Sheila open her presents. Everyone is waiting in the recreation room for you to arrive. It is really crowded and getting kind of hot there."

She looked at me with a look of disbelief, and asked, "How long have they been waiting?" I replied, maybe, "20 or 25 minutes. Come on let's go, they would probably rather get back to partying or might have already done so." I was hoping I could make her think they had got tired of waiting if they were not there. It seemed like she might have been disappointed that Michelle and I did not have other things on our mind for this evening with Sheila. Reluctantly she agreed to meet us in the rec-room after she fixed another drink. I looked at Michelle and she smiled then said, "If she has another drink she'll pass-out." I came back with, "That's perfect, all we have to do is make sure she has a couple more."

By the time Mrs. Sisslor arrived for the unwrapping process she had finished half her drink. Michelle and I began to make plans to fix her another one. Sheila was having fun receiving gifts. She finally got to mine. It was a very nice silver identification bracelet. Mrs. Sisslor took the opportunity to say, "How nice of you Patrick, now she will always know who she is. Even if she forgets, all she needs to do is look at her bracelet. That is a perfect gift for Sheila. You do know she forgets things all the time. I am actually ashamed of myself to have thought you might have something else in mind for my little Sheila tonight." I replied, "Yes ma'am Mrs. Sisslor, I know she tends to be forgetful. It must be a characteristic you handed down to her with the beauty. It seems, my dear Mrs. Sisslor, you have forgotten your drink needs refreshed. It is almost gone, and the ice is totally melted. What is your pleasure ma'am? I shall fix you another one."

A short time later, Michelle and I found Mrs. Sisslor lying face down on her bed in the master bedroom wearing only her panties and bra. For a short second I thought about bringing her to sexual consciousness with some pleasurable foreplay. I knew the amount of alcohol she had consumed would be working in my favor for the partaking of her pleasures. Michelle would not allow it.

She looked at me with kind of a pissed-off smile and said, "You have a private bedroom birthday call to make, and I don't think you will have enough time for a dual performance. Besides, if you wake my mother, you will not live long enough to present Sheila with what we have planned for her."

Other kids at the party were busy doing party things so we knew they would not miss us. Once we were all three in Sheila and Michelle's room, we locked the door. The honor of presenting Sheila with tender pussy pleasures was going to be a joint effort from Michelle and myself and we wanted to take the time to do it right.

Michelle got things started with the juvenile innocence of touchy-feely on me. My hands became an extension of hers on Sheila's nervously sensitive but eagerly awaiting body. I leaned down and kissed her on the forehead and slow-traveled my teasing tongue to her ear. Michelle was administering a soft rolling body massage to her gorgeously tasty looking nude form.

Once the pussy pleasuring presentations started and Michelle became the tender loving care and reassuring love giver for both Sheila and me, the bubbles began to burst. I had just started my journey in the exploration of Sheila's mid-land of marvels when Michelle began to handily gesture my family jewels. That process appeared to be helping Sheila relax. Probably just knowing Michelle was involved as a pleasuring partner provided a healing process for her nerves.

For some reason Michelle seemed overly anxious to assist me in providing the tingling sensations of traveling fingers on Sheila's mouth to middle torso. She was paying special attention to her esophagus and lips. Suddenly I felt my prick growing and crawling into an uncomfortable position in my pants. Since mine and Michelle's penetrating pleasures did not include sexual intercourse, I had not prepared my mind for interference of this nature. Consequently, I was required to make an immediate mental adjustment as well as an adjustment for the comfort of my cock.

Michelle noticed I was having a bit of a problem. Being as

eager to help as possible she immediately gave my pecker a couple fast jerks then abandoned that project. She quickly moved to the other side of the bed and sat down. This put her on one side of Sheila and me on the other side which allowed easier access for both of us to perform the functions we had planned for Sheila's pleasures.

Sheila started smiling. I think she realized I was experiencing an interesting bodily function that had interfered with the attention I had been giving her. I moved up and gave her a short tongue to lip surfing kiss and whispered in her ear. "Happy birthday Sheila, that distraction was all Michelle's fault. I am going to make you this birthday promise. It will never happen again. From now on I guarantee you, sweet little Sheila, the three of us will be coming together as one. If Michelle decides to handily gesture me, you are also invited to do the same. If I should start a finger tapping pleasure prepping process on Michelle's titty's, you are also in possession of two very scrumptious looking little titty nipples. Please know that I have two hands and a mouth with a tongue that is starving for the flavoring taste of your nipples. Now, if we are both forgiven, though you may not realize it, your skirt has already been unzipped and your panties removed. Isn't Michelle good at what she does? While I have been occupying your earlobes, she was preparing my path for pleasurable play time with your sweet little edible virgin pussy."

I gave Sheila a sample of nibble-nipping her chin, followed by a little kiss peck while Michelle and I were very gently moving her sweater up over her titty's. Michelle had zipped Sheila's skirt up so she would be able to quickly cover the exposed bare essential parts of her body in case their mother woke up and knocked on the door.

I kind of leaned back a little so I could get a better view of those bare essential parts. I took one look and my temperature started rising along with other parts of my anatomy. I could tell from the look in Sheila's eye there was a nervous excitement taking place at the point of no return just below her tiny little shiny flat tummy. Her inner thighs and love nest instigated a movement of invitation. Her gorgeous little bellybutton began to speak to me in the language of love. As I laid my hand on the inside of her thigh Sheila's body movement spoke for itself. With very little effort from me my hand became the covering for her soon to be eaten little virgin pussy. With that move Sheila took charge and formulated a plan of action for my attack on her attractions. I was not in control, but I was right where I wanted to be. I was under the influence of her body talk. She reached down and got my left hand and placed it on her titty as she was lifting her tummy towards my lips. Then she treated my right hand to a soft squeeze of occupancy and introduced my fingers to the outer edges of her pussy lips. I lowered my mouth to her tummy and tongue traveled her soft-silky-like skin to her bellybutton where I installed an internal lip lock. I released it with a snapping-pop and began a tongue traveling walk-wash to the window of opportunity at her vaginal canal opening where she had been occupying my fingers.

Michelle had been playing her part very well. She was performing a soft stroking massage to all possible uncovered parts of Sheila's body. But that was just with her right hand. She kept her left hand openly occupied and squeezing almost every part of her own torso while gently whispering soft words of comfort to enhance all of our pleasures.

I started kiss-licking my way around the most connecting parts of Sheila's thighs. I found her to be very blessed with a protective barrier of pubic hairs. This would of course be to my advantage because of the excitement minor pain presents. The questionably sensual and sexually induced pussy pain of pubic hair pulling with one's lips somehow entices the early arrival of climaxes. It also helps to deliver strong orgasmic bliss.

It appeared that we were well under way with the presentation of Sheila's birthday present. I, however, was having somewhat of a problem keeping my mind on Sheila being sensually and sexually satisfied with a happy state of mind landing. It had become too easy for me to glance over at Michelle. She was presenting an exciting performance that was tempting me to watch. She may even be intending to distract me from the pleasure of partaking of Sheila's oh so edible pussy. Michelle had allowed herself, either intentionally or accidentally, to become overly concerned with her own orgasmic desires. She had permitted her fingers to find places on her body that I would like to replace with my own. Michelle had also begun to share the juvenile tackiness of sticky youth-filled juices of her vaginal parlor with her sister's nipples and lips. I had suddenly developed a lust on my lips for the taste of Michelle's youthful love lava. I guess my eyes delivered a message both Sheila and Michelle received. What the hell is going on here, that should have been for me. All of a sudden Sheila's body movement became a loudspeaker delivering silent screams for the unquestionable possibilities of a magnified early release for an internal explosion. Her sexual senses were being overwhelmed by the type of attention she was receiving from both Michelle and me. I immediately lost my lust for Michelle's love lava and went back to work delivering Sheila's. That process took little more than the touch of my tongue to her twat. The couple seconds it took for my tongue to achieve entrance was more time than Sheila needed to erupt. ***She pleasured my tongue with a controlled spraying spread of her virgin-ness. So soft, sweet, and sticky was the lava of Sheila's love.*** It left an aftertaste that certainly took and still holds a very special place in my wonderful world of afterglow.

Having achieved our objective of bringing Sheila to a birthday climax brought a smile and tear-filled eyes to all our faces. Especially since our worries of an unexpected interruption by their mother did not take place. That gave me reason to rejoice. Knowing how well Michelle understands her mother's ability to control her alcohol content indicates the possibility we will have much more available time to enjoy the pleasures of love's treasures.

I would think it goes without saying, Sheila's birthday party was a success for all concerned. That would include Mrs. Sisslor by succeeding in the process of inebriation to the point of no return. She was a very nice lady and I believe in my heart of hearts that she knew something was up and she had those extra drinks on purpose so she would be able to sleep through it.

Chapter 3

"Separate Ways"

****

SHEILA, Michelle, and I were so close over the next couple years everyone referred to us as the Three Musketeers. If one of us were to show up at an event you could be sure the other two would be around somewhere. We quite possibly could be found in a closet or a vacant bedroom, maybe in the basement or garage. I seem to recall one time the three of us found our way under the porch at a friend's birthday party.

Over the next couple years there were many times we used our togetherness for exploring the process of loves pleasures anyway and anywhere we could find enough time and space available. We of course had our own definition for closeness and enjoyed the full swing of our three-way love affair as often as possible. It carried us through our graduation and lasted until we all went our separate ways in life. Then 5 years later at our class reunion, we held a short continuation of what at that time we could refer to as our menage a trios of a marvelous and meaningful memory lane fling. After that I guess we all felt it was time we gave our lives apart a chance. I am not sure, but I believe they were both married and live in Ohio.

I was not married yet and lived in the nation's capital. On any given day I could visit the Washington Monument grounds or the reflection pool and surrounding area and have lunch with as many different young ladies as you could count for the rest of your life. It was for sure the only place I had a desire to be. The females outnumbered the males by 5 to 1. They were mostly government secretaries and lived close by in Maryland or Virginia.

A good friend of one of my uncles owned a driving school in

that area. My uncle had called him and told him I was going to be coming to see if he had any jobs available. He was a very engaging gentleman and informed me that he did have jobs available for driving instructors. He further informed me that my clientele would be 95% female between the age of 16 and 35. With a very large smile on my face I asked, "Could I fill out an application please?" He responded, "By all means, I knew if you were anything like your uncle that would help you make your mind up." And I became a driving instructor for the next 50 years. It was a perfect job for me, considering the areas I was most concerned with were my clientele and monetary status. I met a lot of very nice people and over the years made many good friends. The more important ones were always the ladies. Since my student base was overwhelmingly female, I knew the more I worked the more possibilities would be created. Consequently, I enjoyed their favoring pleasured presence on an average of 100 hours per week. I would usually try to arrange my schedule so the one I wanted to have dinner or go out with would be the last student of the day. It did not always work, but more often than not, it did. I met lots of great ladies and wonderfully beautiful girls and made a lot of money. Sometimes the combination of the two just seem to go together. I thoroughly enjoyed every day of it and plan to open another school before I cross over the great divide.

Fortunately, there were very few requirements for that position at the time. I picked up my very first student two days later in northwest Washington, DC. She was a very nice lady about 55 years old. Her name was Mrs. Jackson and she had never driven before. I had been driving on the farm with tractors and old trucks since I was probably five years old and just naturally thought that everybody had some idea of how to drive. That, however, was not true. I found out very quickly not to take anything for granted, especially in the driving arena. This job was obviously all about, on-the-job training.

Mrs. Jackson got in the car, and we made our introductions then I said, "Mrs. Jackson I am not familiar with this area so let's make a right at the stop sign and we will try not to venture too far from home." She immediately hit the gas and turned the steering wheel to the right, and we became motorized pedestrians on the sidewalk in front of her house. I was able to bring the car to a halt without sitting on her lap just before we hit a tree. I very calmly said, "Mrs. Jackson, could I use your telephone?" Extremely nervous and very apologetic she told me I could. I called the driving school office and identified myself then asked the receptionist if I could speak to the office manager. The office manager transferred me to the area supervisor who had no idea who I was. To be very honest, at that time, I was not sure who I was. After a minute or two, we finally got it all figured out. He informed me they were getting rid of that car and the dual controls had been disconnected. He further indicated he had no idea why it was assigned to me.

I was very eager to let him know just who I was and tried to remain calm while doing so. I verbally rendered my introduction and conversation with the owner, along with the owner's friendship to my uncle. Which, over a short period of time, my explanation and his understanding ways resulted in me being home-based out of their Virginia Foreign Car Driving School division and was given a brand-new Volkswagen beetle to teach stick shift on.

My relationship with that supervisor never developed into anything more than cordial. Even after a couple years when I was promoted to area supervisor and became more informed on the ins and outs of the driving school business. There remained an easily identifiable lack of association desire. I had nothing at all against him. I thought he was a good supervisor and driving instructor, however, I believe he might have been a little unhappy with the way I had originally expressed myself.

I was glad to be working out of the Virginia division and got along very well with that area supervisor. His name was Dwight. He and I had similar ways and similar ideas about how one should live their life to be happy. If the truth were known Dwight probably had his own little world of afterglow to fall back on from time to time.

I can still remember the very first student I picked up in Virginia. Dwight was riding with me so he could include me in his weekly report. He prepared a different report for me than he did for our office files. The report he prepared for me was delivered in what turned out to be our local meeting place. It was a beer joint, or bar and grill in Arlington Virginia called the Hickory Chick, a quaint little place where most of the driving instructors and off-duty Arlington County police officers congregated to discuss the daily events. Dwight verbalized me as a pussy-hungry lady's man, who probably wouldn't know what to do if he were to be taken up on all the complementary proposals he makes to his students. He went a little further while critiquing my performance by saying, "Parsons, let me know how that one works out for your schedule. I'm ready to take her off your hands anytime. You do know she wants you!" I looked at him, we did a bottle clicking toast and I said, "Yes sir, I do know that. She made it abundantly clear just a few minutes before I came here. I will put your offer on the list just in case her husband does not stay out of town enough or gets too suspicious. I don't like violence."

I had been working about three weeks as a driving instructor and made my normal late-night pitstop for a beer at the Hickory Chick. Somehow it seemed the most popular event discussion of the evening usually turned out to be about Parsons and his women. Without sounding like a braggart or unappreciative, I would like to say the owner, my top boss, had been totally honest with me. I had no male students on my schedule at all.

This all took place a few years before the schools had a driver education mandate effective in either Maryland or Virginia. To my knowledge DC has never had a driver education mandate. The event being discussed pertaining to me, and my student's interaction was placed at number 11, and probably should have been 15 or 16. For one reason or another there was a small number I probably could or should have pursued with a little more vigor. Maybe I will drop back on them at a later date. Who knows, they may become a necessary commodity.

Chapter 4

"Grass Skirts Tell Tails"

****

The person being referred to as my student was a very beautiful, and rather petite 26-year-old lady from Hawaii. She would be pushing it to weigh 95 pounds, and I am sure she was under 5 feet tall. She could walk straight up to me, open her mouth and give my nipple a nice little tongue massage without stretching up or bending down. She could almost walk under my arm. Her name was Christine and she lived in Chantilly, Virginia.

On her driving lesson that day, we had stopped by my apartment in Annandale for a pick-up on where we left off from her last lesson. Which included a different type of driving instruction that I was just beginning to make available for needy and interested students.

I still have visions of her grass skirt tap-dancing on me in the bathtub with nothing on under it. As she was making her way up my body from her last landing point, which you should know without me telling you. I believe the word point might help you identify the body part. To get back to my conveyance, I am sliding down to meet her. I propped myself up in the tub on my elbows and she squatted to her knees. Pleasuring my mouth tongue and lips with the lusciousness of her warm wet spread open fabulous female flavor. There she delivered a very enjoyable, tantalizing temptation for me to make myself comfortable by entering her pleasure filled pussy parlor. Christine was arousing my sexual senses in a way I had not experienced before. She performed a pleasurably viewing and entertaining slow-motion shimmy shake butt bounce. Back and forth, across, up down and around my chin and lips.

Displaying perfect pussy lip muscle control, she gave pleasure to my nostrils with a soft pussy lip squeeze pinch process. I could not help myself. As her grass skirt was performing a short soft ballet on my face, I was mentally, physically, and emotionally, forced to respond with my version of a nose to clit massaging.

Yes, I did keep track of numbers for a while, simply for determining influential memories. When everybody's name is either sweetheart, honey, baby, sugar, or darlin' it does become necessary to put the real name with the number. Especially for proper placement consideration of inception to my Wonderful World of Afterglow. Which as it turned out, Christine indeed was truly worthy and enjoys strong after-glowing status on my wall.

Names are also important to keep from showing up at the wrong honey or sweetheart's house. This only happened once in my 50 some years. I was teaching both adults and teenagers at the time and had five Jennifer's on my schedule. I had one of my adult Jennifer's scheduled for 10:30 PM. When I knocked on the door her mother said to me, "Don't you think it's a little late to be going on a driving lesson? What time are you going to be bringing my daughter back?" As soon as her mother showed up at the door, I knew what I had done. So, I went to the car, got my schedule book, and gave her mother a rather quick embarrassing apology for my mistake. She understood and was okay with my explanation. Just one more reason for names and numbers, as well as the egos of afterglow.

Chapter 5

Cigars And A Southern KUM-fort Shower And My First Shaved Pussy

****

As I recall, my next excursion of after-glowic worthiness took place in Arlington Virginia. She lived in an apartment on Walter Reed drive. As we conversed on our way back to the car, I made my mental assessment of her body characteristics. Everything seemed to be in the right place, and she was put together very well. She was tall with beautiful long flaming red hair and walked with a semi sexy modeling strut. She possessed a powerful strong seductive southern accent that flooded her presence with the flavors of sex. Her name was Alyssa, which in my eyes complemented her appearance very well.

When we got to the car, I opened the door for her and gave a hand gesture for entrance. For some reason she grabbed my hand and held it as she was sitting down. Then she said, "I am not used to this, I will use it to my advantage. I hope you do not mind, but you may use all the good manners you want with me." I replied, "Oh no ma'am, it is my pleasure, and it goes with our company policy. We had no training for teaching driving. The only instruction sheet we were required to read said to be polite and wear a suit and tie. If we fail to comply, we get written up. And the company has a three-strikes, and you are out policy. For some reason it seems to work. I may be wrong, but I think I do a better job of teaching driving under those requirements. Our company has very few complaints and lots of students. As a matter of fact, it is the largest in the country. Should you ever need someone to open a door for you just call me. I will be there with bells on, as they say. Actually, what you see is what you will get. Me in a three-piece suit and patent leather shoes, just for you." She jumped in with, "I will keep that in mind. I never know when I am going to need someone to help me get into my apartment."

As her lesson progressed, we got a little more familiar with each other through normal conversation. I found out she was from Atlanta, she found out I was from southern Virginia. I found out she had been married for 2 ½ years but suddenly decided she needed to be free. She got a divorce and moved to the Washington metropolitan area. She found out I was single and liked it that way. I found out she was 31 years of age and she found out I was almost 22.

I noticed it was about 8 PM and almost time for her driving lesson to be over. I said to her with kind of a surprised tone in my voice, "Alyssa, time is really passing fast this evening. I guess that old saying, time flies when you are having fun, is true. We better start heading towards your place. I wouldn't want to cause you to be late for a date." She looked at me and smiled then said, "I wouldn't want to be late either, if I had one." I thought to myself, we were only a couple minutes from the Hickory Chick. Maybe she would like to have a drink. Besides, those guys need something else to talk about. They don't have enough excitement in their life, which is kind of sad. I have no problem if they need to fill their minds with what they think I am doing, besides, it is an ego builder, so I asked her, "Well, how about this? You do not have anything to do, and I do not have anything to do. Why don't we grab a drink and do nothing together? There is a little bar and grill just up the street that I go to every now and then. How about it, do you want to check it out?" With an I'm not sure look on her face she responded, "Well, maybe just one drink." I came back with, "That's great, since you are my last student, I have a little free time." That was not really the truth, but I called the office and told them I was running late and asked if they could move my next two students to another day. They did not seem to be happy, but they did it anyway.

After we had parked the car and were walking toward the entrance, I felt she should prepare for some possible questions from some of the guys. I told her the Hickory Chick was kind of a gathering place for driving instructors and off-duty Arlington, county police officers. And not to be surprised if people made certain comments about instructor student friendships. I thought she was going to say that she would rather not go in. Instead, she just raised her eyebrows a little and said, "Okay!"

As we entered and made our way to an open booth, you could feel a draft from the heads turning and the eyes checking us out. I guess because I was relatively a newcomer, they were paying more attention. I noticed Dwight was sitting with someone but only occupying half the booth. I asked him if it would be okay if we joined them. They both nodded their approval, and Alyssa and I occupied the other half of the booth. We made our introductions and found it must be an instructor student night out. The party sitting with Dwight was also a student.

I asked Alyssa if she wanted a mixed drink or beer. She indicated the beer would be fine. I ordered a pitcher of beer, and we all began our get to know each other conversation. It kind of seemed like there should have been role reversals. Dwight was in his 40s and his student could not have been more than 25 years old. However, the longer I stayed in the Northern Virginia and metropolitan area it became very obvious to me that a person's age did not matter. I found out, as I will relate to you through my confessions of sorts, that age made absolutely no difference in the dating or sexual arena.

We hung out there for maybe an hour or so before the four of us decided it was time to try someplace a little more interesting.

Dwight suggested we go to the Plaza Seven Restaurant. He said, "They've got a good country band and a dance floor." I glanced at Alyssa with a question mark in my eye. She smiled and nodded her approval. The four of us headed for the Plaza Seven.

Alyssa had two or three glasses of beer while we were at the Hickory Chick and was beginning to loosen up. She was exhibiting an interesting overly anxious desire to be closer. My training car was a bucket seat Volkswagen beetle, and she was damn near setting on the gear shift. What an unravelling twisted conversation that could have inspired. Although I will say, a few years ago in my hometown I heard about this young lady that had been given a dose of Spanish Fly while watching the movie at a drive-in theater. Her date went to the concession stand to use the bathroom. When he returned to the car, she had locked her pussy up tight on the knob that screwed onto the end of the gear shift lever. An interesting way to get off! Was it true, was it false, or was it hearsay? Spanish fly apparently was a form of drug farmers gave their animals for breeding purposes. I do not have any idea, you decide!

We had been at the Plaza Seven for about an hour or hour and a half and had a few more drinks. The girls had gone to the restroom, Dwight and I were discussing possibilities. He said to me with a kind of grin on his face. "Man, I thought she was going to rape you during that last dance. It looks like you know where you're going to be spending the night. I bet you're glad she's divorced." I replied, "She does act a little hungry. Maybe the divorce is a good thing. I have not learned everything I need to know. Alyssa is a little older than I, and she is hungry for love and attention. I might just consider this one the beginning of another training program and let her have her way with me. I will let her teach me where to go and what to do when I get there. You know, kind of like putty in her hands. I think she might like that. I know I would because I know she has been to a hell of a lot more places and I have. And *I want to learn what she knows, once she takes off all her clothes. I bet she can put on quite a show, and my friend, you can be sure I will let you know. Just how deep our hunger goes"* Dwight came back with. "I wish I were your age again. I don't know what the hell I'm going to do with this one." I said, "Make sure you teach her something she doesn't already know. She is looking to you for an experience so give her one. Play that funky music and take her places she has never been. Next week, transfer her to my schedule for a lesson or two and maybe she will teach me what you taught her. That is what I am all about. I feel I must learn something new on every one of my escapades. Dwight looked at me and said, "You are one crazy bastard. You do realize you are the instructor, don't you? I know for sure you are fucking nuts if you think I am going to let her get anywhere near your schedule." I jumped back in with, "But Dwight, you are my supervisor. Just think of how much faster I could learn what I need to know if I were taking lessons from both of you at the same time. You and Alyssa, I know, are so far ahead of me when it comes to the sexual arena. It boggles my mind just to think of how much knowledge I could acquire if I were being trained by the two of you at once." Dwight looked at me with a very questionable and strange look on his face, then he said, "Boy you must have been born sideways. And you probably should go right back to where you came from as fast as you possibly can if you get my drift. Because I can tell you right now, that shit ain't happening." About that time the girls returned and inquired as to what we had been talking about. Alyssa said, "I saw that strange look on Dwight's face, so I know it must've been something interesting." Dwight responded with, "Nothing to be concerned about, just a little under the table instructor talk. Parsons seems to think he needs more experience. I told him to keep his head on straight and he'd be all right." Alyssa sat down beside me and said, "Patrick, I think you are a very good instructor. After all you got me this far away from home and that has not happened in quite a while." Then she nudged me with her shoulder and kiss- pecked my cheek as she whispered, "Now all you have to worry about is getting me back home. I think we should have a couple drinks for the road since we have so far to travel. Oh, by the way, I know you are my instructor, but I really don't think I should be driving." At that point Dwight's student spoke up and said, "I know Cynthia is not going to be driving home. I doubt if I could even start the car, much less drive it." I jumped in with, "Your name is Cynthia. No-one introduced us and I was wondering what your name was. Much like Alyssa, Cynthia is a very pretty name. Do you go by Cynthia or Cindy?" She came back with, "Either one will do, I'm not particular."

Chapter 6

"Cigars a Southern KUM-fort Shower"

And
("My First Shaved Pussy")

I looked over at Dwight and said, "Two gorgeous ladies with beautiful names, man, what more could we ask for." He nodded and tipped his glass to what I had said then replied, "It has been a great time with good company, but I think we better be getting these young lady's home after this drink." Everyone agreed and the girl's kind of semi-hugged while Dwight and I shook hands and said, see you later.

As we approached the car, I started to open the door for her. She somehow managed to get between me and the door and began to administer a rolling body massage accompanied by a lip lock that almost extracted my tongue. I guess the last beer was having its way with her senses.

We finally got seated. Seat belt laws were not in effect at that time, but I always tried to wear mine. Alyssa put a stop to that right away. She leaned over and unzipped my pants and gave my prick a couple squeezes and a jerk. Then she looked up at me and said, "Oh look I found a cigar. I just love cigars, and White owls are my favorite brand. Does Patrick mind if I smoke his White Owl on the way home?" I gave her titties a soft squeeze and rolling elbow massage while I was shifting the gear lever into reverse and quickly replied. "Baby you just make yourself right at home because that's where we are headed. I just hope we get there safely." Alyssa's head was bobbing up against the bottom of the steering wheel from the overly aggressive suck-puffs she was applying to my hard as a rock make believe cigar-cock. Dwight was right, she was pretty damn hungry. I busted my nuts before we got out of the dam parking lot.

Alyssa lived about a half a mile to a mile away and never once lost her loving lustful cigar connection on the way. She just kept inhaling and never choked on my smoke. Which fueled my curiosity and made me dream a little as to what she had in her little bag of tricks for the rest of the night.

Once we fondlingly found our way into her apartment the first thing she did was fixed us both a drink. She was definitely a Southern Bell. Her drink of preference was peach flavored Southern Comfort with no mixer. I didn't know about her, but I knew I had to watch what the hell I was doing, or I was not going to last long in my world of coherency. I might turn into bedded down peach seed.

We finished our first drink without spilling a drop while body surfing our way from the couch to the floor. Alyssa got up to fix another drink and announced, "I believe I shall take a shower would you like to join me there? Oh here, carry my drink, I think we better take the bottle with us just in case we need it." She never gave me a chance to say yes or no but that was fine with me because I just followed her shaking little bouncing butt right into the bathroom. Where we immediately took another drink and exchanged it through a kiss. I guess that is what you would call a Southern Comfort mouthwash.

It took about 10 seconds for us to strip each other to total nudity. I had no idea what she thought about my body, nor did I care. **The very first thing that caught my eye was her pussy had no hair. This was a first for me. I had never had the pleasure of servicing a shaved pussy. It quadrupled the excitement streaming through my mind and body as I shot my first round on her shiny tummy and watched it drain down onto her hairless twat.** She looked absolutely delicious! Alyssa quickly dropped to her knees and performed a satisfying lip to penis main vein draining massage. I suddenly felt my heartbeat speed up accompanied by a teasing tingle in my nut sack. My tongue got hard, and ***I inherited a stiff-dick-hard-on from hell, this Georgia peach was ringing*** *all my bells;* I am sure my heart was heavily influenced by the Southern Comfort. All I could think about was starting to devour her entirely. And it did not matter where I started. *Her toes, her nose or the nape of her knee, her tits, her belly-button or her wet little pussy; Her armpits, her shoulders or the back of her neck, her inner-thighs were so sexy my mind was a wreck; With the whole of her body my mental did flirt, Then I decided Alyssa would be my dessert; She slid the shower door open and we both stepped in, Alyssa was wiping cum-drops from her chin; She lip-sucked each finger then said with a smile, grab a bar of soap we shall bathe for a while;* She immediately began to busy herself by sudsing up her entire body. I, of course, followed and admired her desire for cleanliness. By the time I reached my mid to lower groin area she had already begun to rinse off her voluptuously shiny, entertainingly edible anatomy. Alyssa reached over and took the soap away from me and continued her own little interesting application of soap suds to any section of my body that might be blessed by sexual activity. Her yearning for cleanliness included what you might term as a sensual trio of sexual sudsing. Which meant three very thorough applications to my cock and balls along with an extremely interesting and sudsy-three-rim-reaming job to my anal orifice. When Alyssa finished, she handed me the soap and said, "It's your turn Patrick." I obliged her with much pleasure, as it turns out, for both of us. My cock started drooling again before I could insert the bar of soap between her pussy lips and entrance to her love parlor. The sounds Alyssa was making were directly related to her body tremors. I believe she was also pleasured by a couple exciting excremental mini blasts. **More commonly known as clit-squirts, or pussy juicing's.**

It turned out to be the most interesting shower I had ever been pleasured with to this point in my life. Our bodies were soapy, shiny, and so slippery. Our fingers had no problem finding a hiding place, which was kind of new to me. I had never been privileged by receiving so many different digits with a sudden sudsy point of interest for penetrating my anal cavity. Alyssa would no sooner get the bar of soap in her hand before she dropped it to fulfill the desires of another digit. Over the next 10 or 15, maybe 20 minutes she knocked my cock stiff and blessed it orgasmicly several times just by opening my back door. I had no idea how she made it happen, but I was very proud of my youthful enthusiasm. Through an unexplored phase of the evenings early events verification was given to my need and desires for Alyssa to become my sex instructor. From that point on she had her way. I did not care what she did and wanted her to do everything she wanted to. I did not care where she went or what she took with her. She seemed to be of that same mindset with me. I do not think from that point on five seconds passed without one or the other of us sucking on something or puncture pleasuring other openings of our bodies.

CHAPTER 7

MY BALL-BUSTING/PRUNE-BONDING SEX INSTRUCTOR/STUDENT

****

SOMEHOW it seemed our animalistic characteristics surfaced, and we were rolling around on the floor of the shower performing all activities of sex except cannibalism. If the truth were known, if that would have been possible, we probably would have accomplished it also. I was on my back and Alyssa was pleasuring herself topside. The shower drizzles were attempting to use my nostrils as a drain, but I did not care. If they had accomplished their goals, I would have drowned happy. Alyssa raised up and slammed her pussy hard down and around my cock and groin area. I felt my prick pushing on the inner walls of her pussy. She scream-grunted and fell forward crushing her tits on my chest. Alyssa then applied a lip lock worthy of tongue extraction. With her body talk and muscle she let me know she wanted to play the old switcheroo. During our travels she grabbed my ass cheeks and pulled allowing one finger to fondle my anal opening while indicating she was hungry and wanted something to eat. She had already prepared my plate with that scrumptiously slap hungry pussy of hers. I was just hoping she would be happy with the snack I had to offer her. Alyssa was on the bottom which allowed me total penetration control while traveling through her sexy lips and over her tongue in search of her throat which presented a whole different world of unexplored pleasures through esophagus travel. While I was enjoying the pleasures of cock-riding the rib cage of her esophagus she had filled my ass hole with her finger and was rubbing my main vein from the inside of my anal cavity. What a hell of a driving lesson. I could feel it happening but there was nothing I could do about it. My nuts exploded and flooded her happy trail. Alyssa coughed a little but paid it no attention, she just kept on sucking my cock and butt fucking me with her finger. What a training program she was giving me. I had been paying so much attention to what she was doing and how she is doing it that I was almost committing mouth to pussy assault by trying to crawl inside. I wanted, hell I needed to become a permanent fixture in her pussy parlor. Suddenly in the back of my mind was a memory I had from years ago. When first I ever partook of edible pussy pleasures and was soon referred to as the best little cunt licker in town. I was having mental déjà vu all over again. I wanted to be inside Alyssa's pussy forever.

Suddenly Alyssa relinquished my cock. She grabbed both of my hands and placed them on her titty's then said to me, "Why don't you try to titty-fuck me while you are eating my pussy? That will give my tongue the pleasure of exploring your body parts." As I leaned forward, the attention I was paying to her tits with my prick forced my butt a little farther up in the air. Alyssa immediately tried to swallow my balls. I could feel her rolling them around from one jaw the other. As she pulled her head back to allow my balls to slide over her lips, she applied enough suction to cause a slapping pop then immediately recovered them and repeated the entire procedure. This time when she released them, Alyssa introduced me to another first with her traveling tongue from the bottom of my nut sack following my ass crack to my prune. There she began a new tradition of tongue to butt-hole bonding. Now I realize why she was so intent on sudsing up. Alyssa was going after my ass hole like I would go after her pussy. Tonguing, reaming, and sucking of the anal opening was all part of my new training program. She was one hell of a sex instructor. I became overwhelmed and immediately fell in love with her. Alyssa reminded me so much of a babysitter I had once upon a time. That was how I felt about her also.

We continued our shower of sex by sucking, fucking,

pinching, biting, and nipple nipping, Alyssa did mine as well as I did hers if not better. When she got through with my tits my nipples were hard and red as the head of my cock after she got through sucking it.

We finally padded each other dry, and she led me to the bedroom. I laid down on top of the covers. Alyssa looked down at me and immediately informed me that she was going to have a White Owl, she liked cigars after sex. As though her newly found White Owl and cigar/cock fetish was not sex. I guess it was something she liked to play around in her mind with and that was just fine with me. I did not care how long she sucked my cock, or smoked my cigar, whichever she preferred.

She was laying between my legs, and I asked her, "Why don't you bring that sweet little pussy up here and sit on my face so I can have some dessert?" She replied "Patrick, you are so young, and you have such sweet meat. I want to suck your prick until it turns purple. Just lay back and dream of whatever you want to dream about. Make it a good dream, think of purple and behave yourself." And so it was!!!

I went to sleep thinking of lollipops, roses, beaches, and purple bikinis. I would be lying if I did not tell you the best part of my dream involved her cigar smoking, cock sucking, sexy lips. When I awoke, I found Alyssa had achieved her objective, I raised up a little and looked down as she took her mouth away from my cock. My prick was hard as a rock and swollen with the favoring of a pale purple flavor while sporting a big bright red head. Alyssa was trying to tickle my backbone from the inside. She had her thumb inserted as far up my ass as it would go. I would have to say Alyssa certainly favored the flavor she received from pruning. And she knew how to make it feels so good for someone who was not trending toward the rear entry pleasures when she met them. Now I do not care what she does. To me it is like she is teaching me the fun and games part for the art of making love. I like learning from her. She makes it all so interestingly personal.

Alyssa asked me, "What time do you work tomorrow?" I

replied, "Fortunately I do not work tomorrow. I do, however, have to drive into the office to make my turn in."

She inquired, "Where is your office and what time do you have to be there?" I said, "The office is on Connecticut Avenue in Northwest Washington, and I have no particular time to be there. Just as long as I am there before they close at 9:30 PM." Alyssa came back with, "That's great, why don't I fix you breakfast tomorrow morning and ride up to your office with you tomorrow evening. On the way back we can have dinner at my favorite restaurant. It is a Mexican restaurant in the northwest area close Georgetown called, the El' Bodegon. That will allow us so much more time to get to know each other and do fun things together. Besides, when you first came to pick me up for my driving lesson you were accompanied by a little voice in the back of my head saying, "Teach him everything you know and don't let him go and until you've got your fill." I came back with, that's fine, but I don't have an extra change of clothes with me." Alyssa jumped in before I could say anymore and asked, "What do you need them for? The clothes you wore when you to picked me up cannot be dirty. You didn't have them on that long. I personally would prefer you go naked around here, that is the way I like it. The calm comfortable warmth of the naked body is much more relaxing to the touch. Being naked also provides the inviting sensuality and sexiness for pleasurable entry with less confusion."

Suddenly in my mind were the sounds of afterglow from Sheila and Michelle maybe she is a relative, so I asked her, "Alyssa do you have any relatives with the last name Sisslor?" she replied, not that I know of, why." I came back with, "No reason I'm just having a few moments of mental déjà vu." She responded with, "I'll bet you are, and I will bet there have been several ladies that enjoy your presence with no clothes on." She smiled as she gently squeeze-rolled my nuts on her way to give me a kiss peck on the cheek and drop a tit in my mouth, first one and then the other. I remember thinking to myself. She may have been married but I do not believe she had any children. Her titties were just too plump and firmly formed to perfection. I almost felt embarrassed for the escaping youthful succulent sounds of an inexperienced driving instructor who found himself trying to perform a masterful mouth to tit massage worthy of their elegant status. It must have been obvious I was unsure of myself. Alyssa quickly took my head in her hands and began a soft mouth, tongue, and lip, move on and across her nipples and down through the cleavage. She insisted on the two-tit process along with a starvingly hungry request for a nipple nip or soft tit bite from time to time. My tit sucking lovemaking massage lesson lasted several minutes. When Alyssa had finished that segment of my sex training program, I felt as she did. That I very eagerly had learned at titty-warp speed. I was ready to display my ability to provide pleasures to any size, shape, or age, tit I might be tempted to apply mouth to nipple satisfaction.

Fortunately for me Alyssa's pussy hunger pains had returned. I had noticed them starting while I was still working on her tit massage. She had placed her body in a way that indicated she might like to try the old standby missionary position. We did just that and it lasted about 30 seconds before she very spiritedly exclaimed, "I want on top!" We rolled over as she physically tried to extract my tongue with her suction cup lips. Alyssa wasted no time, she immediately set up and began to do a rodeo topside rumble. The tit massage must have got her more excited than I had realized. Either that or she just wanted to fuck all night. She was bouncing up, down and reaming around the sides. My prick was standing at total attention. I could feel the head of my cock stretching the inner walls of Alyssa's pussy parlor. I was hoping she would make it large enough for me to insert my head. Perhaps I might find a soft pillow like place in the reception chamber to rest my head on and maybe go to sleep. Then I know I would feel like I was home at last.

Alyssa was still rodeo romping while squeezing my shoulders slapping my face and pinching my tit-nipples. She was scrape reaming the mouth her pussy around the exterior walls of my cock-shaft like she did not have a care in the world. Right at that time, perhaps she did not.

I could not help wondering why she was not concerned about the time. Although I had no idea what time it was, I knew it had to be in the early hours of the morning. We did not leave the restaurant until after midnight. I decided not to worry about it and just let her do her thing. After all, I felt she was putting my time to good use. It almost seemed like from the training I was receiving I should have been paying her.

Almost like she had been reading my mind she said, "By the way, I forgot to tell you, I thought it best if I take the day after my first driving lesson off. You came very highly recommended. You might say, your reputation precedes you." I slowed my pussy grinding ream role to stop and sat up. Then I asked her, "What are you talking about?" She wound up and fired off another round of nitty-gritty, down and dirty, hard fast nut cracking snatch patch pleasers and filled my ass hole with a finger as she replied, "One of your students is a good friend of mine. She told me everything I needed to know about you and your driving desire to learn. She knows me very well and suggested I take the next day off." I inquired, "Which of my students are you referring to?" Alyssa gave me a sexy smile and rubbed her tongue across the protrusion point on her upper lip. Then she surfed my upper torso with her mouth while treating my tits to a tongue washing and semi hard nipple nip. She rather hurriedly gave the upper part of my breast a gully wash and immediately began sucking on the exterior of my esophagus. Then said, "It's a surprise, you'll find out soon enough."

From there we fell into another experimental layer of the lovemaking atmosphere that lasted somewhere between an hour and a half and two hours. I really was not sure if she was just trying to get her money's worth or adding a little pleasurable pocketbook pain to the possibility of sending me a bill for my training program. We visited and revisited every bodily orifice available. We renewed our desire to go deep fast and hard in every position possible. Although her esophagus had become my special place, I was only allowed to spend a few seconds there. I was, however, given an extra minute or two for a titty-fucking, body-shaking nut-buster. I believe it was because Alyssa wanted to make sure my prune had been properly prepped for tongue travel. She really enjoyed that process. It appeared that she was having a series of small tremors while serving up many different samples of shallow surfing my anal orifice. After all those little experiments had been successfully completed Alyssa found comfort and excitement with something new. She took my hand stood up and said come with me Patrick lets experiment with the couch. She instructed me to set right in the middle of the couch where the pillows separate. Then she walked around to the back of the couch directly behind me. She leaned over my shoulder and started massaging my nipples. Alyssa pulled my face around to give me a warm wet tongue twisting, teeth tracing saliva sample. Then she said, "Baby I have got something I've been wanting to try for a while, and under the circumstances of our encounter I believe you would be the perfect lover to provide the right response." She gave me a little kiss peck on the nose and put a nip bite on the end of it. As she followed her tongue tracing down over my chin and on to my esophagus and upper breast area she said. "All you have to do is follow your desire. This is going to be as new to me as it will be to you. Do anything you want to do to me in response to what I'm doing to you, and everything will be fine." She immediately latched on to my esophagus with the master muscles of her mouth and began a fast and furious tongue washing of each exterior rib. It felt like she was trying to get in from the outside.

    Alyssa continued her tongue travel from tit to tit applying several sharp snapping nipple nips. By this time her hand had found my cock. She went after it like she was a hungry sex crazy woman that wanted a mouth full of cock and cum and could not jacked me off fast enough. I was actually a little shocked, at the way she was pounding my cock, but it didn't take her long to succeed in her objective. She had built up an atomic blast in the main vein of my pecker and had snaked down over my body far enough to lick the drool from the head of my tool. Alyssa was crushing her tits on my chest as she applied a violent crashing massage to my lower torso.

She quickly closed her mouth and released the holding pressure on my main vein. I damn near blew a hole in her face. She kept moving my cock all around on different parts of her facial area like she was applying makeup. She turned her face and looked up at me and smiled through the cum-drops falling from her nostrils. Alyssa had made sure to completely cover her face with jack-off-juice. Continuing the jerk off process of my cock with one hand, she used the other hand to gather my excess love juices. Then rubbed it all through her hair and on her body with special massaging attention to her flattened tits. They had been crushed flat against my rib cage while completing their journey down. Alyssa had managed to snake her body far enough down into perfect position for her mouth and throat to become the recipient of total tonsil saturation by swallowing my cock. Her head fit perfectly between my legs and into the pillow separation. Which is exactly what she was trying to do. I think she wanted to make sure the top of her head could go far enough down into the pillow separation of the couch that she could incorporate sucking my balls along with the cock swallowing process. That would also allow her easy access to my ass hole. Alyssa's hips and upper thighs were resting on my right shoulder. I knew damn well what I was going to do. There was no way she could get her pussy that close to my mouth and expect me not to satisfy my devouring desires. And devour it I did. Being mentally geared for total consumption of her scrumptiousness I did not have to concentrate on anything else. Alyssa was more than willing to help position her thighs around my head. My nose even got a little snatch bite. We were not wasting any time maneuvering her completely edible sweet warm wet protein packed pussy for my more than eager mouth-bonding manipulatory pleasures. She placed it perfectly in direct line of fire for my tongue to taunt her clit. What a great position. Her legs were spread eagle. Open wide enough for my mouth and chin to be halfway in her pussy parlor. I went after her pussy at top mouth motor speed, crushing and consuming everything in my path of pleasure. I mean, I gave her a good cunt clobbering and molested her clitoris with teeth tracing suction. Alyssa was swallowing my cock all the way down to the bottom of my shaft. She had pulled my nuts into her jaws on both sides and had not started choking yet. Our position and behavior were so unusual on this particular lovemaking event, I felt compelled to contribute something interestingly strange and different. It didn't take long for me to start thinking abnormally. The atmosphere was perfect for me to make the next move by staying with the theme of unpredictable sex. I leaned forward slightly and placed my left hand on Alyssa's left shoulder and my right hand on her right shoulder. Being as easy on her head and face as possible I started scooting my butt forward. Her mouth ran over, and she unwillingly spilled one of my nuts as she choked a little and cleared her throat. I said quickly, "I want to try to stand up. When I pull up on your shoulders, I think it would enhance both of our pleasures if you would try to squeeze your thighs and hips tighter around the back of my neck." Without saying another word, it was done. We had successfully achieved a standup 69 'er. It was amazing, I do not know if she had ever attempted that before, but I know it was the first time for me, but not the last. I was walking around the room with a bounce in every step and pulling up on her shoulders. With every bounce I drove cock deeper into her upright tunnel of esophagus love. Alyssa responded perfectly by crossing her legs behind my head and squeeze pulling upward. She allowed me enough time to take a breath on about every fourth upward squeeze. It was crazy, she was draining my come compartment and sucking my main vein dry on about every fourth step. Suddenly she dropped her legs back into spread eagle formation. Then Alyssa sucked her stomach in, which dropped her pussy down on my chin, and screamed, "Eat my ass-hole you lovemaking little fucker." It was not like I had a choice, the moves she had just made positioned her, tight but not timid, little anal opening perfectly on my mouth. She was fanning my jaws with her inner thighs as she pumped her legs up and down from their spread-eagle formation. When my tongue penetrated the crack of her ass, she delivered a steady flow of cum-droppings on my chin and started a jerky quivering process. Alyssa made a few moan-groaning sexual sounds of ecstasy with every little jerky quiver. The more I could ream the rim of her prune and the deeper my tongue could penetrate the more Alyssa flavoringly favored my chin with secretions of her love. She was having short little orgasmic bliss-filled blasts while I was tongue fucking her in the ass.

We continued our weight loss muscle building sexual encounter for at least another hour. I have no idea how much weight I lost or how many orgasms I had. One thing I can tell you is the next time we tried the upright 69'er it was a piece of cake. I felt much stronger so I must have built a muscle or two.

We got started on our way to my office in DC around 2:00 o'clock the following afternoon. I told Alyssa to drive because I thought the inner-city traffic experience would be good for her. That was not the real reason, but it was true enough. She had been so good to me by supplying a fantastic sex training program and providing a nice warm body to cuddle with while having a special layout for literally intermittent creamy dreams. I thought I could somehow repay that favor by giving her a little free driver training instruction.

****

Chapter 8

"Our Rock Creek Parkway"

(Driving/Sex Class Exhibition)

****

I finished with my business at the office, and I thought we would drive back through Rock Creek Parkway. The scenery was better and there were occasionally places to pull off and park. I only had to pull off one time to find out what was really on Alyssa's mind. We had walked around to the front of the car and was standing with our backs to the road when Alyssa made her first physical statement. She gave me a kiss as she unzipped my pants and grabbed my cock. With a soft low screaming squeeze, she exclaimed. "I want it now!!!" I replied, "I thought you wanted to stop for dinner." She very quickly informed me that we were stopped, and she was about to have dinner, or at least an appetizer. My back was to the road. Alyssa dropped to her knees and proceeded to lighten my load. I tried to camouflage the situation as much as possible but finally realized my efforts were fruitless. I put my hands on the back of her head and began fucking her in the mouth. Alyssa began to savagely suck the head of my cock. I responded with rapid fire abuse to her tonsils. People that were driving by realized what was going on. Some of them blew the horn and yelled, "Yeah, yeah, or sock it to her man." I guess one of them saw the driving school sign and yelled out. "Now that's what I call a real driving lesson." Along with other interesting tidbits of acknowledgment.

Our next stop was the restaurant she wanted to go to. It was pretty cool. It had a roving minstrel and a waiter that went from table to table squirting wine in the customer's mouth. He had very good aim, the only way he spilled the wine was if you shut your mouth. By the time we had a few drinks and dinner Alyssa told me very plainly what she wanted for dessert. She further informed me that it would have to take place in the shower first. I liked her addiction to the cleanliness of sex.

While we were on our way home our conversation consisted of, as you may have already guessed, sex. As to the why's and what for's, of some of her preparation to past positions for added pleasure. I was driving because Alyssa wanted it that way, so she could busy herself at play. And that is just what she did. She was building my cum compartments content to maximum capacity. I believe she was doing so because she liked watching my uncomfortably pleasurable, jerky movements brought about by the delivering of a **cum "mother-load."** Her prepping process was almost 100% successful except for a constant drip of cum from my slow drooling tool. Speaking of tools, the tools of her trade were her tongue, tits, fingers, and her cock wrapping fist. She used them all to the point of perfection.

I was driving on Columbia Pike in Arlington Virginia being accosted by a sex maniac. Alyssa had her finger up my ass and was massaging my nut sack and lower shaft with the palm of her hand, thumb, and forefinger. Oh, by the way, did I mention I had my choice of which tit to suck on and nipple nip. I wonder if anybody thought it might be strange the way the car was weaving around. But after all, I did have a driver education car with student driver signs on it. We somehow arrived at Alyssa's apartment alive and hungry for more. Both of us were harboring severe hunger pains that were causing mental confusion as to the whereabouts of the shower. Alyssa was trying to make sure we wasted no time on our way to the shower. She already had my belt unbuckled and my trousers open. She pulled them down and hurried me in the direction of the bathroom. I reached up to unbutton her blouse and tripped over the foot stool. We both hit the floor with our hands full. I had kept hold of her blouse as my hands were trending downward. They brought with them her bra, panties, and skirt. We hurriedly helped each other to naked as we crawled together into the shower.

The droplets of warm water from the shower were splashing off our bodies from side to side. We lay perfectly fit together in a very satisfying 69'er with Alyssa in total command of her favorite cock swallowing topside position. The hunger pains started subsiding after about five or ten orgasmic blasts on both our behalf's. We continued to roll around from wall-to-wall with warm water adding to the orifice excitement for each point of entry we made. Alyssa seemed to be possessed with the soaping up of all private parts, especially the ass-hole area. She did the soapy finger cleansing procedure on both our butt holes. She actually spread her pussy lips and swallowed the entire cake of soap while sudsing up. She definitely liked clean!

Alyssa stretched up and took the personalized body shower nozzle in one hand. I could not help myself. The way she had stretched her body out of any kind of normal contorted form was sinfully sexy to look at. Her entire upper torso was pulled out of proportion and one tit was stretched almost totally across her breast area and flattened except for the nipple and overlay. The other one remained the same. I raised my body to my knees and my mouth went straight for the nonexistent tit's nipple and started devouring it. I had no explanation for why my cock went immediately to attention status. It was like I felt I must restore the disappearing tit back to its original titty status. I pulled it into my mouth with the power of hickey suction to the nipple and overlay. This continued much longer than normal, and she never tried stopping me. She had taken the handheld nozzle and was thoroughly hot and cold, hot and cold, inner pussy wall rinsing the whole time I was in my, I think I'm going to eat your tit mode. I finally noticed her moving around a little out of the ordinary. I looked down to see what was going on. She was masturbating by applying the nozzles vibrating water mode to her clitoris. Alyssa was sitting with one hip against the shower wall and leaning on her shoulder and butt. I am not trying to be sacrilegious but I always kind of like the term, "my rod in my staff will comfort thee." I had seen enough.

She had struggled by almost losing a tit. Now she is

attempting to replace my pleasure stick with the water-pick. She looked as though she was in need of comforting. My cock was standing straight up and ready to administer all the comfort she could handle, or at least that is what I thought. So, I made my favorite statement and reached down to push the nozzle away from her pussy. I pulled her body out away from the shower wall and mounted her sidesaddle. I rather abruptly threw her left leg up over my right shoulder and with both hands on her hips I totally filled her with my comfort bone. I had been taught this position a year or so earlier by one of my other lady friends. It supplies the leverage needed for the penetrating pleasure pole to completely achieve pussy parlor invasion with wall stretching pleasure pains. Alyssa became very appreciative for my interest in comforting her and reciprocated by involving us in another 30 to 45 minutes weight loss and muscle building program. After which the hole soaping process started all over.

We finally found a couple very large towels and dripped our way to the bed. There I began, still under instruction, the padding dry process of Alyssa's entire body.

Once I had semi-dried everything except my favorite lounging parlor, I drifted back there with the always present mental and physical desires to crawl inside.

Alyssa was issuing her padding instructions from a propped-up position with two pillows behind her against the headboard. Her legs were somewhat spread eagle bringing my view of a perfect pyramid topping to be the entrance of her wonder world. The view was mind boggling perfect and I began to dream. My mental reception for the lips of her pussy, was swinging doors to the entrance of a very picturesque perfectly shaped pussy pyramid. I was in a semi-stable state of spellbound pussy consciousness. I stared at her invitational swinging doors that could possibly allow me permanent residence in her perfect pussy pyramid. Suddenly I had an after-glowing moment from high school history class about people being buried in the pyramids of old. **That is all it took, I wanted to crawl inside and die there. My pussy padding took**

on a mind of its own. I went rogue and uncontrollably began to prepare for my inevitable demise between her thighs where my soon to be home lies.

I believe Alyssa realized she was wasting her breath with instructions. I had started an unconsciously overzealous prepping procedure for my, soon to become imaginary tomb in her womb. I knew I had to get it wetter so that I could pat it better. I began a trip with my traveling tongue that took me to Paradise. The inside of her thighs was of course the exterior walls of the pyramid. I tongue traveled those thigh walls to the pyramid pussy point and crossed over to the other side. There with full extension of my tongue I began a tantalizingly tormenting treatment to the doors of her pyramid pussy by slurp slapping and swinging them open wide enough to crawl inside. There I found a glorious little bell to ring while totally devouring her clitoris.

Alyssa had forgot about the instruction process and was enjoying watching me take the initiative to make an ass out of myself. She must have known it was not going to work. Perhaps somebody else she knew had tried it once upon a time and also failed to complete the perfect rhyme.

I started coming back to my senses and my mind returned to normalcy. I realized I had totally saturated her pussy platform and now must proceed with a vigorous padding-dry process to rescue her drowning scrumptiousness. Having acquired enough pussy packed protein to perform the process at the highest level, I began to apply my long-delayed topping of temptation. I tongue traveled from side to side to outline her pussy perimeter. **Then I pamper-prepped her warm wet pulsating pussy to perfect pre-climatic behavior with a tender teasing towel tap-dance finger-rolling pad-dry on her proudest possession of pleasure**. Alyssa was pleased. She was letting me know with every little jerky quiver provided by so many orgasmic blasts. Rendering her clitoris and the inner lips of her wetness tender to the touch. I added a blow-drying soft finger flip process to bring more pleasure for her treasure. I had no sooner added a cold blowing blast of air and fingertip touch to her clit when she screamed, "Yes-yes-yes, oh yes, that's right, that's right, do it again baby, do it again, do-it-- do-it—do-it, till I die-die-die!!!" and saturated my teasing towel. Alyssa grabbed my head with both hands and pulled my mouth hard into her pussy. She began a bouncing delivery of mini orgasms for appreciation on my tongue and said, "I didn't teach you that." Then yelling between screams of satisfaction and squalls of saturation she exclaimed, "E-U-U-U-U, You Are Good, you fuckin' little hillbilly!!! Pour some Southern Comfort in it and slurp it up from my loving cup. You are so good you deserve a drink from my high-class thigh glass. Where did you learn that?" I replied, "I just kind of figured that if I gave your pussy and clitoris a little cooling down blow-job they would feel better to the touch." Alyssa grabbed my cock and screamed, "Christine was right, you are just too damn good to be true. I am going to eat you alive. I think I'll start with your cock." She gave a couple demanding body jerks on my cock and we fell immediately into what had become our favorite pastime position, you eat mine and I will devour yours, a ("69'er.")

After giving my entire cocks head several full rib rides in her esophagus, she lip-washed and tongue traveled her way through my butt cheeks to my ass hole. Then using both hands she spread my butt apart. With a little help from a thumb roll, Alyssa privileged her tongue to plunging penetration. She used a seesaw move with her nose and chin between my ass cheeks to ensure as deep as possible tongue reaming. I was on the other end of the (69'er) with my tongue and thumb providing the pleasantries of a masseuse to her clit and pussy area. At the same time, knowing how into rear entry Alyssa was, I took the liberty of delivering a pleasurable two knuckle deep middle finger bung-hole bonding blast to the reception lounge of her anal orifice. **She went nuts!!! I Mean Haywire, clearly over the edge, with what must have been a rectal release. One of her favorite pleasure responses. Alyssa immediately relinquished control of my ass–hole and started slurp biting my entire shaft. She took total control of my mind and my body by grabbing my nut sack. She was forcing it to** serve as a rope to pull my cock up and down over the rib cage of her esophagus. Alyssa was using seriously sexy force that turned into a rampaging rumble with bodacious intent for nut busting on every rib of the innermost parts of her oral tunnel of love. She was having some serious fun along with sadistically oriented thoughts of sexual domination.

That sure as hell was a first for me. That's what I like about this place. I have learned so damn much in such a short period of time. I tell you something else I learned. You never know how willing you can be to move your body around until somebody grabs you by the balls and starts pulling. I got so damn good at it I was moving before she started pulling. If I hadn't been I believe she would have pulled them off. And there ain't no such thing as a *"NUTTLESS WONDER!!!"*

I think it goes without saying the remainder of the night evolved from unusually strange acts of sex into the wee hours of the morning's discussion about the why's and what for, and how much we both enjoyed whatever.

CHAPTER 9

"DUAL GRATIFICATION PERSONIFIED"

****

THE next day I found myself in serious need of sleep. I called all my students and was able to cancel all of them but one. She was a very nice 41-year-old student. She had set up 12 lessons over the next two weeks. One every day except on Sundays. As she was adamant about keeping her lessons close together. She felt she would learn faster than if they were not spread out over a longer period of time. She indicated that unless it was absolutely necessary to cancel, she would really like to keep her lesson this evening. Since her reasoning was good, I agreed and asked her if she minded if I made it a little later, maybe at 9 o'clock instead of seven. She told me that would be fine but to try to be on time.

That gave me an extra couple of hours to sleep. I figured I would be okay with that considering that was the total amount of sleep I had in the past two days.

By the time I got a bite to eat, took a shower and went to bed it was 11:30 AM. I slept until six, got up took a shower and shaved, got dressed then went to pick up my student.

Her name was Margaret Connor and she lived about a half hour away in a nice middle-class neighborhood called New Dover. It was a subdivision of Arlington Virginia. I arrived about 10 minutes early. She must have been sitting at the window watching for me. When I pulled in the driveway, she opened the door and came out to the car.

I greeted her with, "Good evening Mrs. Connor. How are you this evening." She replied, "I am fine but in kind of a hurry to get started on this lesson." I noticed she was walking with a limp, and

I had not noticed that before on any of her lessons. I held the door open for her to get in the car and apologized for having to move her appointment to a later time. She said, "That is not why I'm in a hurry, it is the nosy neighbors. I wish there were no signs on your car, then they would have something to really talk about. They are just a bunch of busybodies. Could you drive until we get away from my house?" I agreed to do so and replied, "You know, one thing I have noticed since I came to this area. People living in a subdivision are little more interested in who is coming and going than ones who are living in apartments or townhouses. By the way, I noticed you were walking with a limp are you alright to drive." She said, "Oh sure, I just turned my ankle as I was trying to move away from the window a little faster than I should have. But it's okay, if you don't mind, I will just sit on my right foot and use my left foot to drive with." I said, "But Margaret, I mean Mrs. Connor." She interrupted me with, "Just call me Maggie, everybody else does." I said, "Okay Maggie, in case you had forgotten this is a stick shift and it takes both feet to drive. However, not to worry, a new driver can always use a little extra work on their steering and shifting. So that is what we will do for this lesson. Then you will not have to be uncomfortably sitting on your foot. I will point out the sound of the motor for you that tells you when you should consider shifting. Look at the little marks made between the speed numbers on the speedometer. That lets you know what the maximum performance of that particular gear is. It is better for the car plus you get better gas mileage if you can shift at a lower speed, unless you are trying to build speed fast. I will tell you when we need to shift and use my hand to guide you through the gears until you learn the gear pattern. I will make it as easy as possible for you. All you ever really need to do is follow my lead and put your hand on my hand on top of the gearshift when I tell you it is time to shift. After a couple times going through the gears, we will do a hand reversal role. This means you will be shifting, and I will be guiding you."

Mrs. Connor looked at me and said, "I have a better idea, why don't I just have a set of dual controls put in my car and hire you to ride along with me every place I go. Then I will always know I have my hands in the right place at the right time since it seems to be all about hand placement." I laughingly responded, "I would certainly be happy to accommodate you ma'am, if it would fit in my schedule. However, I believe you are going to be just fine. I am sure we will know after this evening is over and you learn the gear pattern because the shifting process is like walking.

Left foot up right foot down, if you stub your toe when you walk you will probably grind a gear every now and then. If you stumble and fall every now and then you probably will do considerable damage to the gearbox. Maybe even need to have it replaced. I do not believe that is going to happen.

I have watched you walk. My dear Mrs. Connor, excuse me, Maggie, you have impeccable timing. And I think you walk just fine, even with a limp. As your left toe leaves the ground, your right heel touches down. Therefore we refer to the shifting process as a walking motion."

In about a half of a mile, we pulled into a parking lot, and Mrs. Connor got into the driver's seat. She adjusted her position slightly, then as she took control of the steering wheel said, "Mr. Parsons, you seem to be very observant, do you watch how everybody walks?" I said, "Maggie, much like you, I would prefer you call me Pat. In answer to your question, I watch all my students as they walk out approaching the car. By doing so I can usually tell if I am going to have a hard time teaching that student to drive a stick shift, it all depends on their timing. I much prefer to watch my female students as they approach. They have a very interestingly smooth body move with every step. Female students make much smoother stick shift drivers than male students simply because of their timing. Men stub their toes all the time. Look at their shoes, they get all dirty, they do not look where they are stepping. I think it is the same thing in life. Women like to know where they are going, and men don't give a damn. They are like a blind hog. They go after everything in life with their eyes wide open in her mind closed. As you can probably tell I do not like to teach guys that much, especially adult guys. They always think they know more, or they know it all. But it very simply goes right back to walking. You do not see very many male models. I believe it just goes with my theory about women are wonderful and men are morons. There are all kind of stats to back up these theories. 80% of men pick their nose at red lights. 80% of women put on makeup. That particular stat says it all. I know damn well which one I would rather watch. I would much prefer to see you pucker your lips in preparation for a phantom kiss, while watching yourself in the mirror as you tenderly molest a very lucky tube of lipstick at a red light. The thought of comparing those two offsetting characteristics only reveals one's intelligence level and would be an insult to you. Therefore Maggie, I shall refrain from doing so. I will remain very content with watching you pucker up and walk with a mini limp.

I do not know if I have answered your question, but I do take a great deal of pleasure in assessing somebody's walking motion for determining their ability to steer and shift at the same time. That is just one more reason I am happy that most of my students are female. Take you for example Mrs. Connor, I am sorry, Maggie, you carry yourself very well and you are put together nicely. You walk with rhythm and timing in every step. You put yourself on display. You unveil your class with every move of your body. This is a gift I enjoy getting from you on every lesson. I do not wish to exchange that for what I would receive from some guy who stumbles and falls all over himself and picks his nose." Maggie started laughing and said, "Pat, could we pull over and stop for a couple moments? I believe I need to gather myself while I digest what you just told me." I said, "Sure, there's a 7-11 right up the street. I'll get a cup of coffee." She said, "That sounds good, I'll have one also."

We pulled into the 7-11 parking lot, and I asked, "Would you like me to fix your coffee for you?" She replied, "That would be great. I like mine with one French vanilla creamer. And just make it a small coffee." When I returned to the car with the coffee Maggie smiled and said, "Thank you very much Pat. Would it be alright, and do you have time, for us just to sit here for a minute and drink our coffee? We can talk a little bit about your flirtatious delivery and the mental gift of women walking toward your car?" I said eagerly, "Absolutely my dear young lady! That is the type of conversation I would certainly always make time for, welcome, and enjoy having." Once again, she smiled and asked, "Young lady, Pat, how old are you?" I replied, "Should I answer you truthfully, or the way I would answer anybody else?" She said, "Both but save the truth for last." I said, "Okay, I can be as young or as old as you would like me to be. Or how old would you like for me to be? Or I am old enough to know better, but too young to resist. Truthfully, my dear Maggie, I just recently turned 22 years of age, and I am trying to learn everything I can as fast as possible. Around the time I was five or six years old I seem to recall my life's needs and desires switching to the fast lane without signaling, and I have been there ever since.

She wished me a happy belated birthday and talked a little about everything that we had discussed except driving. I finally said, "Maggie I do not know if you realize it or not but, much to my dismay, you were doing all the steering and shifting without my guiding hand. I was beginning to think you would be leaving me sooner than I thought and how much I would miss you when you are gone. She replied, "I wasn't even thinking about it. I guess I just fell right into it from doing what we were doing. Our conversation made me very comfortable and happy." I came back with, "And that makes me happy. Maybe if we get into another good conversation, I can talk your ankle into not hurting." She replied, "You already have, I have not even thought about it until just now but it's not hurting at all. Of course, I am not walking on it either." I responded, I am not sure I could talk the pain away, but if you were of a mind to give me a chance a little later, I bet I could make it stop hurting. She looked at me with a Mrs. Connor questioning look on her face and said, "Patrick, I am 41 years old, and you are 22. What in the hell is wrong with you? Or maybe I should ask what in the hell are you trying to do?" I replied, I am not a doctor, and I don't have any pills. I do not like to see a lady in pain. I thought maybe you might have a pain where a pill cannot reach. If the pain were to go away it would be an extremely desirable learning experience for me to have such a pleasurable opportunity of learning from a teacher like you. Just knowing, somehow you had turned me into an instrument of comfort in your life, would serve as comfort to me as well. I told you I am trying to learn everything I can as fast as possible. If I were to have my way, I would like to have the experience of 100-year-old man by the time I am 23. And **you, my dear Maggie, are loaded with all the charismatic characteristics, charmingly desirable mental makeup that proudly lays claim to your voluptuous exterior's arrival. You walk with the whispering hint of educated sexual encounters that my mind and body crave. I could not ask for a more perfect specimen of female flesh to honor me by administrating my sex training program. I will make you one promise. It will not matter where it is or what you want me to do when I get there. You need only tell me once and I will make it happen for you."** Maggie had this look on her face that just kind of explained the night away. I knew from that look what she had on her mind was the same thing I had on my mine. Here we go with the stars again!!!

She began her next verbal delivery with, "I have had a pain where a pill could not reach or even take the edge off ever since the first day you showed up at my door to pick me up and teach me to drive. All dressed up in a three-piece suit and patent leather shoes. You were looking good enough to eat, with a kind of melt-in-your-mouth but too tender to chew personality, and I knew I could not swallow you whole.

Your introduction made me weak in the knees. So much so, you seem to have this habit of reintroducing yourself every night in my dreams. Good evening Mrs. Connor, my name is Pat Parsons. I am here from the Foreign Car Driving School to fulfill your desire to learn to drive, and you handed me your business card. Your business card seemed to automatically require residence in my bedroom. That evening when I got home back after you drivingly instructed me, I went into my room to straighten up a little. It seems you had your way with me and did not know it. I placed your business card between the frame and the glass of my dresser mirror. And I have had many satisfyingly interesting conversations with you since. Why do you dress like that and talk the way you do? You are a hillbilly! You are not supposed to be talking like that." I came back with, "I guess I could blame you for being a woman. All my life I have been the recipient of women's love. Older women and younger women as well. I just live and love to make women happy and make them feel good. I have always had the deepest desire to make women forget something bad and leave them feeling better than they did when I met them. I guess in a way it is kind of like paying back for having such a good life to this point. Paying forward so it will continue to happen. I never knew a woman I did not love, and I hope never to meet one I do not love. And with the same respect, I never knew a woman I did not want to make love to. I guess I have probably answered your question. Now you know what I am trying to do. And my question is to you, not what are you trying to do, but what would you like to do? Or, better yet, what would you like to have done? I would consider it a great honor if you were to allow me to take that pain away and fill your life with fun. Besides, I like my three-piece suit and patent leather shoes. I have always wanted to talk the way I talk, and not with a hillbilly accent."

    I had the feeling we should finish her driving lesson, so I said, "I suppose I should get back to instructing and finish your lesson. Otherwise, it's going to be kind of late when you get home." She looked at me with a smile and said, "The hell with that, we need to get a motel!!! If you open your mouth one more time with another verbal array of driving desire deliveries, this car will start rocking. Though it is kind of small, the seat has been serving as a holding tray for the internal combustible shockwaves of my comfort zone. You said I only had to tell you once. Patrick, find a place!!! Make it quick or I shall rape you in your driver training car. Now how does that equate to the whispering hint of educational sex your mind and body so desire and crave. I guess we are about to find out if you are full of it, or real. Here, I believe you better take over the controls." **And so it was:**

I immediately turned the car around and headed up Lee. Highway towards Falls Church. Dwight had turned me onto a no-tell Motel in that area the first week he worked with me. It was pretty nice, they also had day sleeper rates and it was very clean, no dust above the doors. I will not mention the name, the owners a good friend of mine. I have coffee with him every time I am in the area.

I checked in at the front desk and drove around to the room. We walked in together and I told her to make sure it's okay. Maggie nodded her head in approval, and I told her I needed to go to the car to pick something up. She said, "That's fine. I need some time to freshen up."

One thing Dwight told me, always be prepared. No matter what, fresh clothes and drinks. You might even want to keep a little some in the trunk to for a snack. This is one job you never know where or whom you might end up with. When I returned, I was carrying a somewhat larger than a regular size briefcase. It was smaller than a suitcase and metal. Maggie immediately asked, "What do you have there, Pat?" I replied, "Just a little something especially for you." She looked at me with a devouringly interesting smile that caused her eyebrows to move almost as much as her lips did when she spoke. I placed the case on the dresser and opened it. I spread it apart to lock it in place so it would stand up. The case was easily identified as a portable mini bar. It was equipped with a bottle of Southern comfort and two personal size bottles of champagne. It had a compartment with several loose cubes of ice accompanied by two glasses. Last, but not least, was a double strapped hand-held Swedish massage machine.

Apart from her mouth being open and slightly jacked to one side, Maggie had that same hungrier than ever look on her face and said as she looked at me, "You knew, didn't you?" I replied, "Yes, I knew that I wanted to be with you. I knew, I wanted to make love to you. I knew, I wanted to make your every wish come true.

I knew this because that is what I always want. The difference is I did not know you wanted it to happen also. Now that I know you harbor the same feelings as I. 'Tis my desire dear Maggie, to make you so happy before this night is over you will lose your mind two or three times and I will probably lose mine a couple as well. Together, we will make this a night of memories we both know, will live forever in our worlds of "afterglow."

I walked over a little closer to her to ask her what she would like to drink. I realized she seemed to be in somewhat of a trance. As I got closer to her. I watched the tardiness of her tender tears revealing the evenings story, releasing all the love one finds when sharing tears of joy. I took my handkerchief and padded dry the tears then kissed her. The joy projected in Maggie's face was so desirable I could feel the tingle of an emotional shock wave as our lips met. The time for talk had passed. The night was ours and it was young. We would have lots of time later for conversation. Still fully clad we turned out the lights and walked each other slowly to the bed and put our minds at rest. We enjoyed every second of the lovingly tender times spent in preparation for the act of love we were about to become involved in. Both Maggie and I experienced mental hesitation to enable the time lapsing while removing different articles of clothing to linger. We had no place to be and no reason to be in a hurry to get there. The only place we wanted to be was right where we were. I knew right away this was a loving time. The one thing I had been taught is, one does not rush the times of love. Maggie must have felt that same way. We spent the next couple hours exploring each other's beautiful bodies. Kissing or tongue washing every inch of unfamiliar territory. I took it upon myself to make sure neither of us missed a spot. That seemed to make Maggie happy and help put her mind at ease for having become involved in lovemaking session with someone half her age.

For me it was a very testing time filled with tenderly teasing temptation. Maggie had absolutely no problem positioning me to be the recipient of whatever maneuver she might invent or have in mind. However, she did from time to time show a little apprehensiveness in allowing me to enjoy the pleasures of connecting our bodies from different entrances and angles. She appeared to be a little bashful or ashamed that I would be exploring parts and places that had experienced twice as much time travel. My time of exploration was open for an occasional nipple-nip and tit-tongue twirling, armpit licking and cock trailing, finger dipping and clit rolling for the sole purpose of maintaining proper body temperature. I tried to control my aggressive desires in order to allow Maggie to play the dominant role. That seem to have been working very well until I discovered an incision in her lower torso. It was probably from an appendectomy. Maggie had started this kiss caressing love procedure for acknowledgment of our life's former battle scars. I of course, following her lead made my lips available for the latent consoling of that particular body battle scar. With my mouth holding a sympathy service only inches away from its favorite place to be, I was suddenly overcome with the desire to be allowed a taste test. Maggie had already gifted me with four or five orgasmic mother loads. She had kept my tool in drooling status for the entire exploratory process. I did not think she would mind if I tried to catch up, and so it happened. I had no sooner administered a tapping tongue trip to the door of her open twat than Maggie initiated a body movement so that I would be on top when I took my first bite. **(What a fur burger)** Although it was not necessary, with what little light that was available I could see I had discovered the ultimate **fur burger. Lord have mercy on my esophagus, tonsils, and my dentist.** I had just landed in pubic-hairball heaven. I grabbed hold of both of Maggie's ass cheeks in buried my mouth and nose and began to snorkel as I searched the pussy lip lining for the flavored body pleasures released by her clitoris. The instant I turned my tap-dancing tongue loose and touched her clit Maggie favored me with a bountiful blessing of desert and immediately started the engine to her E train. She administered a very talented Afterglow slap-happy tongue whipping to the rim and head of my cock then started my timber member on a bouncing back and forth trip of her esophagus. All at the same time I was collecting saturated pubic hairs. They are so much more excitingly enticing and tasty when flavored. If you are really good at collecting them, you can strip the flavor off as they try to choose which tooth will be there home. I have formed a nice little pocket in my jaw to store them in. Maggie has so many if I am lucky, I might be able to collect enough to make a little pincushion for her to remember me by.

We had been performing the esophagus travel and the pubic hair collection for quite a while. I know I must have busted 437 nuts to go along with the constant drool of my tool. I think I managed one for each time I hit an esophagus rib with the head of my cock. Maggie's cum holding chamber must be about to run over. From the response of my throat and pubic hair collection chamber I thought I might have collected enough to achieve my pincushion memoir. I started letting my tongue and fingers explore other areas for pleasure seeking. As I began the lubrication and reaming process for possible entry of Maggie's seemingly protected prune, she began to squirm her butt around as though she were trying to get away and say no.

Maggie finally shut the train down and asked, "Pat, do you mind if we have a drink and talk a few minutes? I think it might be a good idea since you are allowing me to play the part of sex instructor if I remain in control." I replied, "Why sure, that's fine I would kind of like to have a drink myself." I got up and walked over to the so-called bar and turned around to ask her what she would like to drink. I noticed she was just sitting there with her hands crossed in front of her in her lap looking around. I said, "Are you looking for something Maggie?" She said, I'd like to have something to throw around me, this makes me a little uncomfortable." I walked over to the closet and got a blanket off the shelf and brought it back to her and said, "I'm sorry it bothers you for me to see you like that because I like it. You have a beautiful body, and you are very beautiful lady. I would consider it an honor and privilege to sip champagne from a belly button of the perfection such as yours. Or ravishingly molesting your armpits with a mouth full of Southern comfort. But if you choose to hide your treasures and limit my viewing pleasures there is one thing, I want you to know. My dear Ms. Connor, I love your body every fraction of an inch of it." Her response to that was, "I would like to think you meant that. You are so young, so solid with no hanging parts. Your entire body spells and omits the smells of sex. Your penis has been erect since the beginning. You are a bundle of sweet meat which I intend to eat as much of as I possibly can before this night is through. Tell me Patrick, we've born with a hard-on?" I did not respond, instead I unfolded the blanket and wrapped it around her shoulders and sat down Indian style on the floor in front of her. I picked her feet up and laid them in my lap. I dropped deep in thought as I was massaging her feet and toes. I wondered if anybody would ever understand the way I felt about women's bodies and their body parts. After a few seconds I lifted her feet up a little and kissed them both, stood up and looked at her and said, "Thank you Maggie, that's the nicest complement anybody has ever, or could ever give me. Now, what would you like to drink?" She came back with, "I think I'll try Southern comfort I've never had it before." I said, "You will like it, it is very smooth but be careful, it sneaks up on you. I'll be right back with your drink but first going to run by the bathroom." I went to the bathroom and picked up two bath towels. One I draped over my shoulders the other one I wrapped around my waist. As I opened the door and walked toward the bar Maggie looked at me and said, "What did you do that for? I told you how much I liked it." I smiled and said, "If I am not mistaken, I believe I told you almost that exact same thing." I fixed our drinks and walked back over and handed Maggie her drink. I proposed a toast to us after which Maggie asked, "Is your penis still hard?" I kissed her on the cheek and said, "You make me feel so young, I guess next You are going to want to bring out the saltshaker. Well until you do let us play that old game I used to play way back when I was four or five years old. I'll show you mine if you show me yours." She smiled and said, "Okay!" Then reached up and pulled my towel away and hung it on my, rock hard love-stick. I leaned in and gave her a little mouth to mouth with slight tongue action as I reached up and unwrapped her blanket and dropped it on the bed. I stepped back a couple steps to admire my unveiling, moved forward and dropped immediately to my knees. With my drink in one hand and her body in my other I performed a short molestation on her bellybutton and tongue traveled her tummy to her tits. I took a short drink and introduced her nipples and overlay to the taste of Southern comfort. Then I gave Maggie a little kiss peck on the cheek and asked. "Shall we cover or do we remain in our wonderfully natural state of nakedness. She smiled and kind of squinted a little and said, "It's okay, I guess." I took the time to hand travel the entirety of her nakedness, paying special attention to Maggie's buttocks and bellybutton. for some reason they really became of interest to me. I suddenly found myself in a very sexy turned on daydream. I was standing at a table where Maggie was positioned on a platter surrounded by flowers. She was laying kind of on one side and hip, with her pussy open and her knee propped up. Her foot was resting on the mid to lower calf of her other leg. She had this seriously sexy look of a wanton on her face and her tongue was slowly massaging the protrusion point in the middle of her upper lip. She was blowing me kisses and requesting my presence with her finger. Maggie's hand dropped to her pussy then trailed her tummy up to give her tits a couple flavored finger soft squeezing massage moves. I had strapped the Swedish massage machine on my hand and started walking toward her. When I came back to reality, I had pushed Maggie down on the bed and was somewhat savagely mouth molesting her armpits. I looked at her and said, "Wow, that was great, you are one gorgeous hunk of female flesh. Now where would you like to sit for our conversation." She looked a little puzzled then said, "Are you alright, where in the hell did you go?" I replied, "I just took the best trip of my life. An unbelievable visual display of your gorgeously naked body. It was great. You said you wanted to talk a little. Where would you want to sit and converse? I think I need a drink. Would you like another?" Maggie handed me a glass and I walked over to the bar to prepare our drinks. I thought I might as well carry the little Swedish tool back over to the bed, I might be able to use it on her foot later. As I handed Maggie her drink, she asked. "What do you have in mind for that thing Pat?" I replied, "Why don't you just kind of lay back to the head of the bed and enjoy your drink while I see if I can take all the pain in your foot away?" I was a little surprised she had no objections. She displayed her body at the head of the bed in a partial sitting or leaning back laying position, with a slight leg spread and lifted her foot up as though to say, here it is, have your way doctor.

I had consumed almost all my drink because I knew I was going to be busy for a while. I knew it would have time to affect my thoughts of pleasuring Maggie and hoped it would help me figure out why I was producing constant come juices while entertaining sensual thoughts about her bellybutton and buttocks.

I had been performing a soft massage with the Swedish machine on her foot, ankle, and lower calf for a few minutes. Maggie had not shown any signs of having the desired conversation she mentioned earlier. My tool had been doing its normal drool, so I decided to gather some wetness **and examine the healing powers of cum** on Maggie's foot. After a minute or two of transferring the slow dribble droppings from my cocks cum dispenser to the wellness program I was administering to Maggie's hurt foot, she started a slow toe massage on my nut sack with her other foot. I looked up at her and she blew me a kiss then said, "That feels really nice and looks yummy, and sticky. I think you should use more. I know I need more." and handed me her glass, then continued, "I want to enjoy all you have in store, to keep my ankle from being sore;" I went to the bar and fixed us both another drink and as I handed Maggie's drink to her, she put her other hand on my cock and stroked it gently a couple times. Then she said, *"Shower my body with what you process, massage me with your stickiness. From head to toe and please do not rest, until you have covered both my breasts, with the healing powers of your yumminess, once achieved I will be obsessed, and eagerly we may explore,* *what lies behind the hidden door, of one thing you can be sure, my ankle will be no longer sore."* With that introduction I stood up and began my performance. Maggie was laying on the bed massaging the protrusion point on her upper lip with her tongue while performing gentle self-pleasure with one hand for her titty's and the other for her pussy. It seemed as though every time I gave my cock a stroke she swallowed. I imagined the movement in her esophagus to be from my excrement's as it bouncingly roll-flowed over each rib of her throat. Maggie must have been caught up in dreamland also. Then, she would smile and provide tummy moves with short breaths to add to my excitement. I was so glad for my youth. This would not have been a good time for my come container to go dry. Maggie could not deny her desires any longer. She reached up grabbed my cock and begin to suck me off. She was sucking so fast and feverishly it was sending little pecker pains all through my scrotum surroundings. Maggie was acting as though she were dying of thirst and was sucking a good slushy through a straw. She wanted it all in her mouth right now.

    I looked at her and smiled as I tipped my glass and proposed a toast to poetry, then said, *"I love poetry, intimacy can be so much more fun, if poetry describes what is being done; I am glad for poetry you have a taste, 'twould be a shame for us to waste; the words describing a picture of, when you and I were making love; here's to love and here's to you, here's to what we're going through; you painted a picture of your desires, now I shall set your world on fire; Lay back dear Maggie, do not try to rise, the miracles of love have no disguise, let your body receive its due surprise, relax your mind and spread your thighs, there I shall prove before your eyes, miracles of love do not come from lies; Your request is for a body shower, for that request you give me power; As your body gathers the dripping drool, from excitement you bestowed upon my tool; when you are covered with my stickiness, I will massage your lovely breasts; Your titts are the perfect size, and shall receive a nice surprise; Your titty-fucking will begin, to keep the cum off your chin, open your mouth, dear*

Maggie, let me in:
I knew I had to get something started but unsure of what it should be. After my daydream, and our presentation of poetry pleasures, backed-up by five or six Southern Comfort's I wasn't sure if I was in Disneyland or Arlington. I think I might have had one too many drinks on an empty stomach.

Trying not to appear as though I just returned from a weekend at St. Elizabeth's Hospital. I removed a towel from my waist that wasn't there, then preceded to folded it nicely as I laid it on the bed. I must've had an interestingly happy look on my face because Maggie looked at me and said. "Pat, if you are looking for your towel it is up here on the pillow beside my head." She was laying partially on her side with one knee up in the air and her right hand almost totally inserted into her pussy. Like she was trying to arrange the entrance and chairs for setting accommodations for an upcoming performance in her pussy parlor. I have no idea where all these thoughts were coming from. It was just kind of like I felt I must be in the reception lounge of some ballroom or Coliseum.

Damn, I guess the Southern Comfort must have crawled up the back of my neck through my Cerebellum and Medulla-ablongatta and jerked a knot in my reality chamber. I knew I had to respond to her comment about my towel. I looked at her with a shit-eating-grin on my face, under the circumstances it was the only kind of grin I could come up with. I replied, "Maggie my dear, the thoughts and desires I am planning for you and your beautiful body's entertainment, along with the unbelievable atmosphere those thoughts and desires are leaving me with, have succeeded in getting me lost in Lala land. I am only trying to retrace my steps so that I might return to reality and pursue the pleasures at hand instead of the ones in dreamland." At that point Maggie busted out laughing and exclaimed, "Pat, you are so full of shit!" She made sure to keep the hand placed on her pretty little fuz-padded pussy parlor, with its finger on her clit undisturbed. She reached up with her other hand and grabbed me by the prick again. Pulled me over and gave it a kiss-suck on the opening of my main vein at the head of my cock. Then she said, "Let us have another drink and get busy in this bed. From what you have been telling me you are going to have a long hard, and deep road ahead to travel while you are delivering the most important driving lesson of the evening." I think the Southern comfort was getting to Maggie also.

I did not think either of us needed another drink. Maggie had opened the door for it by suggesting we have another so naturally I did my duties and fixed them for us. Maybe it was to help her build a secure feeling in how she viewed our situation since I was considerably younger than her. Another drink may help her close the age gap. I knew the age factor was not bothering me, other than I would have to modify my rate of consumption a little. And that was the part I could not understand because Maggie had two more drinks than I and it did not seem to be bothering her at all. As I brought the drinks back, I said to her. This will probably be my last one, so you will have to let me know, if and when you want another drink. As you mentioned earlier, my dear, I think the good doctor is going to be quite busy exploring possible cures for areas with lingering pain.

I tipped my glass to her and asked, "Shall we get started? What area seems to be giving you the most pain my dear, and why do you think it's happening?" I had taken a very limited sip of my drink, while on the other hand Maggie almost drank half of hers in one shot. That in itself told me what I needed to know. Maggie had to drink to be involved. This might be a problem some men, but it certainly does not bother me, nor did her age. I think that is the reason I was able to accomplish what I accomplished that night. Maggie needed a confidence builder, and I was bound and determined to make that happen, even if I was half in the bag. I knew once we got started it would not take me very long to get back on the right track, if I could entice her to enlighten me on what she wanted.

Maggie's response to my questions were, "Yes sir, I think we should get started immediately if not sooner." and "Oh by the way Doctor, I hurt everywhere in every way. So, while you are choosing where to start, maybe I should choose the part of you with which I'd like to play." I indicated that would be fine with me and guess what she grabbed. With a little friendly persuasion and pulling,

Maggie had me comfortably positioned on my knees straddling her breast area and massaging my balls with her tits while sucking my cock. That indicated to me that most of her pain was mentally self-induced and could be solved quite easily by providing enough juice. And that is exactly what Maggie was working on. She had told me earlier she wanted all I had to provide and that is what I was going to supply.

As my cock was making its gradual moves through the revolving door of Maggie's lips, I looked down at her and said, "My dear, before this night is through, I am going to take every pain away and spread a protective cover of love lava all over you." With that promise I guided my right hand behind me toward her twat for a touch of tasty tenderness. I put my left hand on my cock to assist her lips and mouth in causing the ejaculation she was dreaming of.

I started a rocking and rolling process with my balls on her tits and provided a much faster ejaculatory process for her lips. While at the same time with my right hand, I stayed true to the rhythm of the rhyme with a reaming role of my middle finger on her pussy's inner wall and clitoral surroundings. We were providing a smooth bronco-busting boob-bounce with the regular **(fucking)** motion from my motor to her mouth. Maggie's hips began to pick up speed with a back and forth-up and down rhythm of excitement displayed through her enthusiastic ass-jumps and my finger-fucking pussy-plunges. Her lips were forcefully squeeze-sucking her share of my shaft. I could feel her lower lip hard pressed against my main vein begging for an outpouring of love.

I knew exactly what had to happen to show her I was serious. Holding her interest with several powerful pussy-plunges followed by soft clitoral finger massages with my right hand. I put my motor in reverse and backed my prick out over her lips and began to masturbate in front of her eyes. Maggie very insistently tried to grab my cock with both hands and return it to what she wanted to be, it's favorite resting place, her mouth. I quickly said to her, "No my dear, this is the love lotion for your facial covering. lay still now while I saturate your forehead, shoot out your eyes, plug up your nostrils, and cover your ears." Maggie stuck her finger in her mouth and got it wet. I was not sure just what she had in mind, but as soon as she touched my ass-hole the floodgates on the "ole" Jizzum Trail busted wide open. Maggie's face and neck were covered with an orgasmic charge that must have been building up forever and just hanging out in my cum container until it was needed to make some lady's dream come true. The only thing left for both of us to do was gently massage and rub it in. I backed my motor out so my cock was lying perfectly between her tits. With my left hand and Maggie using both her hands we massaged her face, neck, shoulders, armpits, and entire upper body down to her titty's, with a covering of love's lotion. I must have been slowly coming out of my Southern Comfort zone. That last charge I delivered was giving me tingling bee sting type sensations all through my nut sack.

    I did not really know much about Maggie's past, or whether she had ever been married or not. I was not concerned, I just wondered why a lady as attractive and pleasant to be around as she, would be so lovelorn. Oh well, maybe I will get around to asking her when we have a little conversation later, but right now there is other more exciting and important business that needs to be manhandled by Maggie's boy-toy. I believe it is extremely important to understand how your status equates in a lovemaking session. Once you know how important you are it makes the term **"boy-toy"** mentally **"TOWER"** over Grand Marshall or District Supervisor. I enjoy being their boy-toy. It makes them more enthused about teaching me what their needs are and appreciate me for servicing them. It is also important they know I do not mind being told what to do, some men are not into that. I am very comfortable with it, and once they find that out it provides them with a new teaching tactic that enhances my love making skills. They do not mind playing their part while instructing me in the art of making love. Which is what they should be doing anyway, they are women that want certain needs to be taken care of. Very few men know, and some are unwilling to learn about the needs of women in the art of making love. When they do become aware of them, they are not really interested enough to provide a lady with a full-service lovemaking session.

You must remember the early 60s was before the Women's Lib Movement. A large part of society, including most men, viewed a woman as a second-class citizen. Many of the luxuries afforded to women today were not available or even considered at that time. When it came to sex most men considered a woman a tool to get their rocks off so they could feel good. Then run to the nearest bar and brag to all the drunks about how good they were and who they just fucked. During those years, in our world of afterglow, most men could not adequately describe what a good lovemaking session was. They certainly did not consider it an art. Men's egotistical mindset and desires told them to go in like gangbusters and get their jollies, zip their pants up and leave like the whipped puppy they were. Leaving the lady behind in a horizontal position with unsatisfied needs. Frustrated and horny some women would satisfy themselves. Others might choose to seek solace with the comings and goings of the mailman, the traveling salesman, the milk man, or maybe even a sharp dressed driving instructor.

In the 60s and 70s the number of female licensed drivers tripled. It became so obvious one of the major magazines published an article about lonely housewives taking driving lessons. It seemed as though an extremely large percentage of those females taking driving lessons were being left lonely and lovelorn in search for companionship. Considering the average driving lesson lasted about an hour and a half. These lovelorn ladies could easily accommodate their needs for a companion by learning how to drive. This part of their movement also increased the income for motels. Some of their managers seized the opportunity to become entrepreneurs of their time by initiating **day sleeper rates.** They also became known as **No-tell Motels.** During that same time, many men began to examine the broken off -**Y**- in their-**XY**- chromosome status.

According to Montague, during the evolution of men and women a piece of the males double **X** broke off into **Y** status. This left them with a crippled chromosome and unable to function under certain circumstances. I am sure a lot of women are thanking "God" today, that many men started examining their intelligence level when it came to sex and tried to become a little more in touch with their feminine side. **(Thanks to the 70s!!!)**

If I keep this up, I am going to lead right into the late 60s and all through the 70s, what a great time it was to be alive and loving. I got fucked upside down, sideways, standing on my head, hanging from a tree limb, on a tree limb, and a treehouse, while horseback riding, on top of a roof while watching and waving to traffic driving by on one of the major roads in Great Falls, Virginia. I devoured a pair of hot legs pussy, while she was setting on my shoulder. And that was just to mention a few rather unusual, but pleasurable places to make love. I must get back to Maggie, I have left her lying lonely, and lovelorn much too long. You can read about my 70s later.

The fact they are women, builds the desire in me to satisfy and keep them happy because their wonderful. They bring so much more to the bedroom than we do. Think about it, the man has a cock, and from what I understand it will not stay hard half as long as they need it to so they can properly take care of their lady's needs. In comparison, women have beautiful body parts. A penis and a nut sack cannot compare with the pussy and a clitoris. And they can perform so many-many more orgasmic wonders than that of their male lover counterpart.

I Love the process of visually exploring a lady's body before the art ever takes place. That is why this particular event with Maggie is so special. I was afforded the luxury of that visual exploration in a daydream. Everybody has a preference and I have mine, as long as it works for them that is the important thing. I love to make a woman happy in bed. I like for them to be happy other places also, however the bedroom is my favorite playpen or studio. The sheets on my canvas, our body and love excrements are my tools of the trade. My hands and fingers are my brushes. I have created or been a part of several masterpieces. Some could have been made into Muriel's for a wall. I have always lived for and would love to be a participant in the creation of the ultimate masterpiece for **the art of making love.**

Wake-up

"Maggie"

I've got something I need to do for you!!!

We were still performing a very energetic bump-an-sway version of the rumba with Maggie's butt and pussy. I tried to convince her to just relax, lay back and watch me empty my cum dispenser all over her beautiful sexy body. She had a problem with that, and she told me. "Patrick, it is not that I don't want to lay back and watch. It is all your fault.

You, with your always hard cock and sexy moves, the way you go about making love with your desire to please me. Your solid youthful body with no wrinkles or hanging skin, only serves as an appetizer to my main course, and I want to eat you alive. Can you not understand that is why I feel I must be continually putting my hands all over your abundantly bountiful body of love? And I am not going to apologize. I am going to continue to help you totally saturate our bodies with our love's juices. You have made me hornier than I have ever been in my life. You pushed buttons I did not know I had." Maggie looked up at me with her eyes full of happy tears and said, "So this is how it is going to be. I do not care where you go or what you do, it is okay with me, and I will be there with you. You are teaching me I am not teaching you. You are my doctor, perform your miracles." I slowly rolled her clitoris and removed my finger from her pussy. I brought it to my lips stripping it totally of all secretions. Then I took her in my arms and kissed her. We transferred her love juices back and forth with our tongues rolling them around in our mouths for quite some time, with a patient projection of passion for things to come. The kiss turned into a tenderness that threatened the verbal delivery of I love you.

I could tell she did not want to experience a lip disconnection, so I made the total connection. I initiated the sliding moves my body needed for perfect entry of my cock into her seriously secretion saturated snatch parlor. As my cock and balls became one with her pussy the kiss became so intense hands were going everywhere. Eventually we locked fingers as we had locked lips and tongues, pussy, and prick. We were now truly making loves every move together as one. That very sensually satisfying loving experience lasted a long time. When we finally broke our kiss connection I was on top. I am not sure how that happened. As we stopped moving, I looked down into her eyes and said, "I love happy tears, thank you so much Maggie, this love is for you." Her eyes displayed the happy tears again and I said, "This calls for celebration. I went to the bar and got the two individual bottles of champagne and a couple glasses and said, "And now, Maggie my dear young lady with your beautiful body, you are a fantastic lover. Let us have a toast to our love."

    I poured the champagne handed her a glass and lifted my glass for a toast and said, "This is for you Maggie, for all you do and the way you weave your web of knowledge and lust to perfectly satisfy and supply loves pleasures. You are too good to me. I have learned a lot through our encounter. I have learned you deserve what you supply. Your class of casual instructions has supplied me with a love that goes beyond just making love. A love I will never forget. And that my dear Maggie, is what I am going to try very hard to supply you with all through the night." We drank our toast and I looked around for a fireplace to throw my glass. I didn't see one, so I just set it on the table and turned to Maggie and asked, "Would you like another glass of champagne or drink before we finish putting this body puzzle together?" Maggie looked at me with tears in her eyes and said with a tremble in her voice. "I feel like I should hate you for the way you're making me feel. You are too young for me to have, and I am too old to hold you. I have never experienced anyone even close to you and the way you make love. You make me feel so special. I want to kidnap you and keep you under lock and key so when I have these unwanted, unnecessary lovelorn and lonely feelings all I will have to do is unlock your door and they will go away. This is as close to love as I have ever been, and quite honestly never wanted to be here. But I do not hate you, quite the contrary Patrick. I love the feeling that covers me when you are around. To say nothing of the overwhelming desire I have, to carve you up and consume you in our lovemaking sessions. So yes, I will have another glass of champagne, and I will make another toast to our love." I poured us both another glass of champagne which finished the bottles and handed Maggie her glass. She looked at me with several inquisitively sensual glances at my cock, lifted her glass and said, "Here is to you Patrick, for all the things you do for me with your tortuously twisted, tantalizingly tormenting, terrible taunts of love, and, to your cock that is always hard." With that we tipped our glasses and drank the toast. We sat the glasses down and Maggie said. "I know I am going to have a very empty feeling tomorrow. But that is all right, because I have never had the feeling of complete and total fullness you have allowed me to experience tonight." We were both naked, Maggie reached over with both her hands and wrapped my nut sack and scrotum area. She gave it a couple gentle hello-squeezes and said, "Hell yes, let's put this puzzle together three or four more times before you take me home. I have a feeling I am going to want to schedule more driving lessons than I have already set up. Oh, by the way, would you fix me another Southern Comfort my dear. I should like to suck your cock with my mouth full of Southern comfort. Maybe I can get it drunk and pay it back for what it is doing to my mentality level." I replied, "Yes ma'am, your wish is my command, and my love stick is ready for your plan."

Since it had been predetermined this go-round would start with a swimming lesson for my cock being submerged and soaking in Maggie's mouth filled with Southern Comfort, she requested the bottom position. She felt she could hold the Southern Comfort in her throat allowing my prick to soak longer between short slow swallows. I never heard of a drunken pecker and honestly did not put too much faith in the success of that project. I did however enjoy the whiskey river rolling tongue favor she was administering to my cock's head. I gave Maggie a few minutes of playtime for her experimental inebriation project on what had become her favorite toy before starting my maneuvers. While she was attempting to influence the brainpower of my pecker, I busied myself fingers combing her pubic hairs. I separated them totally all around the outer rim of her pussy lips, making it easier for my mouth and tongue to determine their point of entry. I wanted to give Maggie as much time as she felt it would take to adequately achieve cock-soaking to drunkenness. I knew as soon as I began to enjoy the flavors of her scrumptiousness with my tongue and lips, she would have to relinquish control of her swallowing habits and soaking desires. Thereby almost guaranteeing failure for the inebriation of my penis.

I performed a ballet on Maggie's tummy by teasingly taunting her with a tongue tipping tap dance that favored her bellybutton with a circular sucking massage. I felt reasonably sure that would suggest to her the mouthing activity to her pussy was about to begin. To confirm my intentions, I very gently thumb pressed the outer lips of her pussy while inserting my middle finger for an enjoyable short massaging action for her clit. I made sure to gather enough love lotion to ensure my next endeavor would be almost pain free. With my thumb perfectly placed for entry of her Maggie's pussy. I tested the sensitivity level of her tender touch by performing a tap teasing entry to the outer rim of her ass-hole with my middle finger. Maggie squirmed a little but continued her cock-soaking process. I could not help it, I had to put her desires for lovemaking satisfaction to a test. I did not want to interfere with her present pleasures. I wanted to provide her with what I felt would be a much more enjoyable and pleasurable act of sex. I applied slightly more pressure on my thumb as I press rolled the circumference of her pussy lips and continued the lubricating massage of her prune.

With very little movement from Maggie's buttocks, I felt the time was right for me to let her see the difference between what she was holding onto, and what she was about to receive. With my thumb and middle finger in position and well lubricated, and full muscle force of my right arm I succeeded in performing the ultimate transcendental transformation extravaganza of togetherness by the inclusion of instant double penetration to our present act of making love. I could feel my thumb and middle finger rubbing together on the inner wall cavities separating sheath of her anal opening and vaginal canal. Maggie let out a choking gasp, a tummy tuck, and a body jerk all at once. I made sure my hand followed her body to keep full penetration and fingertip contact inside. She never let go of my cock. For the next several seconds she was performing a head jerking with swallowing gag-choking sounds. Suddenly Maggie took total control of the situation she had been subjected to. She reached up grabbed my ass with both hands and pulled down with all her strength, driving my cock-shaft deeper and deeper into her esophagus, and the race was on. It seemed like Maggie opened her throat and was able to engulf my entire cock-shaft while performing the up and down pulling on my ass to grant me the comforting pleasures of her esophagus rib-cage rumble. I reciprocated by the forceful procedure of fanatically finger fucking her pussy and prune with a gentle finger-tip rub-touch of anticipated connection on the inside.

    Maggie started a move that could have been considered a new horizontal position dance. It was a combination of Jerry Lee Lewis's Whole Lot of Shaking Going on, and Chubby Checkers' Let's Twist Again. She added her own little version of Shimmy, Shimmy Coco Pop. I had not realized she was so into dancing, especially from the horizontal position. All I knew was she was tossing me around like I was a feather while performing her rockabilly bed-time butt-bounce boogie. I like Jerry Lee and Chubby as much as anybody else, but right now they were interfering with my ability to get my mouth in position to perform oral surgery on Maggie's pussy parlor. Every time I thought I could replace my thumb with my tongue she released a shaking-twist, and I grabbed a mouth full of pubic hairs. Her throat, tonsils, and the lower esophagus must have been enjoying their own version of Happy Days. The way she was bouncing around and pushing me up in the air, as I fell back down it seemed like my cock was trying to get to the point it could rub against my middle finger and thumb to add 3rd party presence on an internal triple digit menage a trois to Maggie's sexuality. It was a little crazy for a while. I was afraid she was going to hurt herself, but she was the boss, so I just rolled with the flow, and o-o-h boy, where the flow did go!

I finally quit worrying about Maggie and came to my senses. I brought my left hand down around and slipped it under her ass then lifted it up to my face and held it tight. As I put my thumb in slow motion and backed it out over her already lubricated pussy lips, Maggie greeted my tongue with an orgasmic release of love juices and brought her butt bouncing to a slow rhythmic roll.

Had this event been open for viewing it may have appeared as though we were involved in a normal (69'er). Since I was a part of that formation, I can tell you it was anything but normal. Maggie had me going on a slow-motion esophagus travel. She used both hands to help me back my cock almost completely out of her mouth, then took a deep breath and with a gulping swallow sound Maggie opened her throat and pulled me down forcefully as though she was trying to swallow my entire shaft and nut sack. I could feel her trying to fingure-pack my balls in her mouth on each side. I cannot say for sure, but it kind of seemed like the most experienced part of her sexual activities had been with blow job/cock sucking, because she was really trying to eat some meat. I, on the other end of this unusual act of sex, had been influenced by Maggie's enthusiasm and was doing double duty with my forceful playtime pleasures. I was giving my best performance of substituting my tongue for a prick by salivatingly slurp-licking the rim and inner walls of her pussy. I energetically preformed a roll-crushing massage to her clitoris with my tongue, in almost perfect rhythm with my middle finger's full length rapid-fire in and out release of total penetration and molestation to her anal opening. This obviously painfilled portion with Maggie devouring my cock and balls, along with me, tongue smashing her pussy walls and pulverizing her clit while performing a bodacious butt- hole bond, continued for quite some time. My body part was pretty much pain free with its driving desire for esophagus travel being satisfied. I had a hard time justifying the forceful flavor that could possibly be termed borderline abuse that I had been vigorously applying to both of Maggie's available midsection love holes.

The love juices were flowing free. I, of course with my constant drool along with three or four choking orgasmic overflows I heard Maggie slobber-slushing with while trying to save by moving it around in her mouth. She seemed to have put her continuous KUM cycle in full working mode. Maggie's love lava had overflowed the rims of her pussy and was rolling down the crack of her ass to her anal opening. Or at least I was hoping that's how the lubrication of her ass-hole was being supplied. I certainly hoped I had not penetrated the private playground property of Maggie's fudge factory.

It appears as though Maggie had come to terms with the fact that she was not going to be able to inebriate the head of my penis. Over the next few minutes, the overzealous unnatural flavor of our lovemaking returned to a somewhat stage of normalcy. We actually found our way to the all-time every day, accepted position for horizontal pleasures. Maggie had eagerly claimed the top side. She immediately began her pleasure process with 10 or 15 up and down body-slam-fucks. Maggie also laid claim to total consumption of my cock and balls with her vaginal cavity and crowned herself Queen of my Cock-shaft. She wore it well and was smiling as she superseded all expectations by turning my scrotum area into an orgasmic flood zone with explosive releases of cum excrements. Maggie was totally filled with sexual bliss as she treated me to a lip lock of vacuum cleaner suction that soon consumed our leftover love juices.

We were tongue trailing each other's lips, searching for possible escaping flavor. Maggie reluctantly broke the kiss and looked down at me, once again, her eyes were filled with happy tears. I reached up and finger traveled her lips and said, "Thank you dear Maggie, would you like to have another drink?" She nodded her head yes, then with almost a crying whisper said, "But Patrick, I do not wish to break our connection. Your cock is so, it is in so deep, and it feels so-o-o good!!!" I smiled and replied, "Let us go there together, and I mean together. I have never tried this before, but I think we can make it work." I jiggled my butt around a little so my prick would bounce around on the inside of her vagina to add a little friendly persuasion, then I said to her, "I think you should sit straight up and bounce around a little. I always like feeling the inside of your pussy walls rubbing against the head of my cock when you do things like that." Maggie followed my instructions. She enjoyed it so much she got a little carried away with her bouncing. I finally said, "Now slide your butt towards me and squeeze the base of my shaft with your pussy lips." I could feel a slight squeezing pressure and smiled, she smiled, bent over, and kissed me then asked, "Now what do you want me to do." I replied, "I am going to sit up and I want you to prepare yourself mentally for a feel-good favor to your pussy parlor. When I set up, I want you to put your arms around my neck and give me a kiss. Then wrap your legs around my waist and put them in a scissor lock behind my back." Maggie performed that process without showing hardly any difference in the pleasures that might be taking place. With all her weight resting on my upper thighs and lap area I put my hands on her buttocks and pulled her pussy tight toward me. Then I swung my legs over the side of the bed. Maggie was now slip-sitting on my lap with her legs locked around my waist and my cock securely locked inside her vaginal canal. She had taken advantage of a couple opportunities to let me know that she had experienced the unusual favor of cock fondling activity against the inner walls of her pussy. Maggie had an interesting smile on her face while she was explaining this to me, which told me that she was having fun. I had no idea how much she weighed and did not really care. I knew I was going to carry her to the bar, fix our drinks, and carry her back to the bed. I stood up with a bounce. Maggie's mouth flew open, her eyes got big as she yelled, "Oh my "God"!!!" I took one more step, pulled her ass tight to me and bounced again. When my other foot hit the floor. Maggie's response was similar but this time in a crying tone she beggingly said, "Oh Patrick, you are so good to me, do it-do it oh, ple—ase do that some more." I quickly replied, "Hold on tight baby, we've got a long way to go." And I took three or four quick, kind of jogging steps. Maggie was responding by rubbing her tit's all over my upper torso. She was kissing my face and neck then suck-biting my earlobes. While I was fixing our drinks, I made a few little mini moves with my ass and Maggie was using the strength of her legs to pull her pussy tighter against my shaft. Just about the time I got the drinks fixed she began to quiver. Then she gave a couple moans followed by a whimpering cry. I set the drinks down just at the right time. Maggie had an orgasmic explosion so strong her response almost brought me to my knees. I managed to gather strength enough to carry her and the drinks without spilling them on the way back to the bed. I set the drinks on the nightstand and then turned and sat down on the bed. My feet were on the floor and Maggie was still sitting on my lap whimper-crying while applying a strong suction kiss to my neck, which turned out to be a hickey. I took her face in my hands, held it out from me and ask her if she was happy. Maggie smiled, kissed me on the forehead, kissed me on the nose, kissed me on the lips and then said, "You know damn well, you do not have to ask me that. You know the answer." I said, "Well Maggie my dear, why don't you use your boy's toy to make yourself a little happier. I am going to lay back on the bed and play with your beautiful boobies. I want you to sit straight up on my cock and bounce that gorgeous hunk of female flesh up and down and give your ass-cheeks a rolling wiggle back and forth. I do not want you to stop until you want to stop. When you decide to stop, I am going to slowly devour the totality of your mid to lower torso. I will eat your pussy like it was a bowl of ice cream. Using my tongue as a spoon to secure all your long-lasting lotions of love. By the time I have eaten my fill of your scrumptiousness, I will have tongue-fucked your clitoral weephole until your cum-container has gone dry. You, my darling Maggie, will be lying breathless on the bed, thinking how much I like ice cream and wishing you had more to give. Speaking of ice cream, we will have to try that sometime. Nothing tastes better than pussy flavored ice cream. Your pussy would carry a special flavor with a lasting ice cream taste guarantee if your pubic hair dessert strainer is used properly. You can pack my nut sack in ice cream. If you want, we could make believe the bed is an ice cream sandwich. We could saturate the sheets with ice cream and chocolate syrup, then crawl inside and eat each other to sleep. By the time I stopped talking she had experienced at least two more mini-blast orgasms. I, with the constant drooling tool, might have had one or two.

Maggie was becoming addicted to the wiggle rolling of my prick. It seemed like she had it down to a science. Every time she completed a couple ass-cheek wiggle rolls, she would be blessed by a jump-squirt mini-blast of orgasmic bliss on her next bounce. She was showing her appreciation by digging her fingernails into whatever part of my body she might be massaging at the time of the blast. It had reached the point that every time Maggie was about to receive her next delivery of ecstasy, my ass would automatically take her an 8-inch ride on my up elevator.

Rendering the reception of pleasure much more intense and lingering as she plunged downward on her favorite elevator shaft. Maggie had succeeded in the inclusion of my butt elevation for her scientific rhythmic fucking formation.

She was fantastic, and more importantly she was having fun. Maggie exhibited a glowing look of total satisfaction that seemed to grow with the arrival of each surprise. I had no idea if she was ever going to stop, and quite honestly, I did not want her to stop. I was having as much fun as she was and maybe more. Watching Maggie's face portraying her happiness supplied my body, mind, and heart, with the overwhelming feeling of mental satisfaction.

Which instantly intensified the formulation and delivery of an abundant outpouring of love's lotion.

An unsolicited thought popped into my mind. This was a

wonderful way to get exercise. If this were to continue throughout the night, it would provide a muscle building process in areas of your body that was normally not used to this extent. What a way to diet, **"pussy juice and cock sauce"** could not be fattening. An all-night performance like this might allow me to lose three or four pounds.

Maggie, of course being more explosive than I, would probably lose eight or 10 pounds. Oh well, just a little mental observation to influence our minds and bodies in a good way.

I looked up at Maggie and said, "The next time you feel like pulling another late night-er with me, I will fix drinks and we shall cover our bodies with Southern comfort. Our lips and tongues will serve as wash-clothes. I read about an interesting way a set of brushes like artists have, could be used for applying liquid to the tender hidden parts of the anatomy so one could make sure of saturation for total body pleasure.

That was the beginning of our next episode, Maggie had finally relinquished control of her elevator shaft pussy-pole wiggle-roll. She looked at me and asked, "Patrick, before you turn me into a bowl of ice cream, might I have a little sample of your promises to come for our next late-night event. I am a little thirsty and it sounded so inviting, I would like to have a preview of coming attractions if you do not mind." I replied, "You certainly may, we can improvise with the body part best suited to take the place of the brushes. But first we must make sure our bodies are clear of all leftover love juices. Which means I will be face traveling and tongue searching my favorite pubic hair plaza. All you have to do, is lay back and enjoy. Allow me five minutes to prep the pubic hair straining process for taste testing." I really wanted to get into that fuzz patch. I had talked so much about doing it, I just wanted to be there. Maggie came back with, "I am really thirsty Pat, could you fix me just a short drink, enough to wet my lips. It will double the pleasures I am receiving from you." I agreed and as Maggie rolled sideways from her elevator position, I soft slapped her pussy, grabbed a handful of pubic hair, and performed a three second snatch vibration with my hand. I got up walked over to the bar fixed her a short drink, walked back to the bed, and handed Maggie her drink. My cock was sticking straight out and drooling. Maggie started forming her mouth to fit over the head of my love juicer. About the time she got to it I exhibited a little cock movement muscle control and bounced it around a little on her nose and upper lip before allowing entrance. The second her lips wrapped the head of my prick she received her reward and swallowed. I rather hurriedly extracted my cock from her suction cup lips and said, "Thank you very much my dear, I am glad I had enough left to lubricate your tonsils. Now, might I have the pleasure, of molesting your love-nest while you lay back and watch?" Maggie mimicked me a kiss and smiled, then she took a drink. I reached over got a pillow and said, "I should like very much, Maggie my dear, for you to place your precious perfect little buttocks on this pillow for me if you will." She did so without response. I quickly said, "Now what would really be nice, is for you to spread your thighs wide enough that I might view the pleasures of your treasure." Maggie looked at me as she was rubbing the rim of her glass on the protrusion point of her upper lip and tonguingly gesturing it with a sensual flavor. Her smile revealed a level of confidence that to this point had not been present in Maggie's appearance or voice. Although I was a little pissed off, I was happy to see that. It also provided me with an energetic desire to produce maximum pleasure for her from my upcoming project of pussy clearing, love lotion gathering.

Maggie was positioned almost sit-leaning against the head of the bed. She had a pillow behind her back in one under her ass. I slid my hands into position between her butt and the pillow she was sitting on, this favored me with a tight little butt bun for each hand. She was in very good shape for her age. Maggie's little ass was sort of like a tight muscular bubble butt. She probably goes to the gym every day her whole body favors firm. Maggie suddenly decided she needed to change positions and said, "I believe I would be better off lying flat so that I might assist you with an up thrust of my pussy for more pronounced pleasure." I thought to myself, she is looking forward to this as much as I am. Maybe the joining forces idea is a good thing. She got into position almost right in the middle of the bed. Her head was resting on one pillow at the headboard and her ass about mid-way down on another. Maggie was stretched out flat on her back. She was right about changing positions. Wearing nothing but the gifts of nature Maggie had her arms stretched out to either edge of the upper side of the bed and her legs stretched to the lower corners. The spreadeagle position produced a bull's-eye appearance for her pubic hair covered pussy. That was my target, I had no problem knowing where I was going. Her leg spread had provided a personalized viewing for the point of entry to Maggie's pussy by a split open separation in the middle of her fuzz patch.

Once again, I made a mental preparation with devouring desires, leaving a double dribble trail of drool from my tool on the sheets while attempting to get into position. I scraped some of the cum juices up with my hand. Maggie knew immediately what was going on and asked, "Oh Patrick, you are always so ready. Please bring some up to me for a little taste before you start the clobbering of my cunt and pubic hair pulling process." The next thing I know my ass was against the headboard, and she was vigorously suck-slapping my love muscle and balls. Her esophagus rib cage was being prick pounded and my balls were bouncing off her nose. I was nowhere near where I wanted to be but was having a bunch of fun trying to get there and keep Maggie happy in the process. This position had always been pleasurable for me. The esophagus traveling part of a (69'er) and the upside-down pussy paddling always generated climatic explosions and orgasmic bliss. I was sure if I decided to allow the lure of the "ole" Taurus trait to have top priority, it would only enhance the treasures to be released later from the uncommon world of Maggie's fur burger heaven. With that being the determining factor, I laid my body on Maggie's body, supporting most of my weight with my elbows on either side of her tummy. I extended my feet up on the wall above the headboard, grabbed an ass-cheek with each hand and pulled her pussy fast and with force to my face. This was a crazy position. Having my feet against the wall enabled me to back my ass out and supplied control of the driving force by using the wall as a push off platform. Since it was a new and unusual (69'er) it naturally required more attention. It presented a pure path for the piledriving power allowing deeper entry for the esophagus travel. Maggie was really getting into it. She moved her head around until she achieved a straight down open-mouthed throat with no resistance to prick pressure. Quite the opposite, she was moving her head up to meet me on my downward approach, which allowed her to swallow my shaft more comfortably. We spent the next 30 minutes or so having fun and enjoying the flavor of the new-found friction filled explosive releases provided by this position.

I eventually climbed down from the wall. While doing so I began to feel Maggie's soft cock-sucking hungry-popsicle shaped lips were not happy. She was going through a short session of withdrawal pains as she displayed a reluctancy to permit the release of my cock shaft. Maggie's mouth, tongue, and teeth were letting me know, on no uncertain terms, how unhappy they were becoming with the departure of her pleasure pole. Through the process of savagely-sucking, nibble-nip biting, and tongue reaming, Maggie maintained control of my cock enough for the travel time of another three or four trips through the entirety of her esophagus tunnel of love. She left behind several shiny battle scar-scraping teeth marks, while trying to prove proprietorship of my prick.

Not only did I learn the dangers of disturbing a lady that had a mouth filled with prick and the desire to devour what she was caressing between her lips in lieu of allowing departure, but I could not believe how Maggie made it hurt so good I wanted to stay. Had it not been my priority of preference was to pleasure her clitoris by total consumption of her pussy, I would have gladly remained in submission to the hurtful heartfelt, fantastically masterful, mouthing masturbation process she had been performing.

Still on my mind and unable to dismiss, was the lingering lure of Maggie's fabulous fur burger. With very little effort I established ownership of the position that was to be my claim to fame for the night. With both hands filled with her ass and my eye on the target, my tongue was splitting hairs. Maggie asked me for another drink. I was kind of expecting her to do this. I was not sure whether she needed a drink for her mental state to understand what was happening that evening, or she was just trying to fuck with my mind. This time I brought the bottle over set on the nightstand so she could fix her own if I were busy when she wanted another. Before I fixed her a drink, I turned the bottle up and took a straight shot. Then I fixed Maggie her drink and laced the rim of the glass with Kum droppings from my drooling utensil and handed it to her. She quickly tongue-traced the rim of her glass, gave me a big smile and said, "Thank you!"

I told her she was welcome and gave her a kiss while tickle flipping and pinch rolling the nipples of her tits to hardness. As I continued tongue traveling my predetermined path to a position of permanence for total consumption of Maggie's pussy, I bowed my head and mouthingly molested her beckoning breasts. Leaving a trail of love lotion, sweat, and saliva I circled and double dipped her bellybutton. From there it was, as they say, a piece of cake. I made it a point to faster than fast, but tenderly, tongue wash the entirety of Maggie's lower tummy. I had arrived and was eyeballing the bull's-eye of her prize possession. The split-open-hole between Maggie's legs that led to my possibly ultimate home, her pussy parlor, was literally lying in the palm of my hands. My face was perfectly positioned between her thighs, which fulfilled my desires. Allowing me a position of freedom for perfect mouth to pussy molestation. Surrounded by a higher than average, security fence of fuzz, I put my mouth in an Olympic state of mind and with a tongue tapping bound I broad jumped the protective pubic-hair-hedge. I went directly to the center separation split and began a soft blowing process as I touched my tongue to the outer lips of Maggie's pussy and pleasured her with a split-second teasing twirl to her clit. She immediately let me know how much she enjoyed the cool air flow to her hot-spot by twisting her body enough to grab my prick. Maggie began a vigorous, almost abusive, jerk-off masturbation move on my love-stick. She accomplished her goal of inspiring a non-controlled nut-buster in just a few seconds. It covered her hand and the sheets with an abundance of love juice. She immediately started moving around scraping it up and treating her tits to a sticky jack-off juice massage. This, of course, interfered with my desired perfect mouth to pussy masturbation process. When Maggie moved her body to grab my cock, she also caused negative movement for my mouth to pussy pleasures. I had been looking forward to giving a solo performance on Maggie's magnificent fuzz patch from my first memory of viewing her heavy haired home of tongue temptation.

    I felt compelled to enlighten her on my desires to place her in Lala land by moving in and taking residence of that opening I so adore. I approached her with the possibility of laying back leisurely enjoying my upcoming performance by saying to her. "Maggie, what a great job of oral gratification you gave me just moments ago. You made the hurt feel so good I wanted to stay and let you suck my cock until it fell off in your mouth, or your face, tongue, and throat become one big muscle cramp and locked up tight around my shaft." Maggie got a big smile on her face and her eyes were rolling a little as though she was trying to imagine something like I described happening. I was glad to see the way she responded so I continued with. "I have a big favor to request of you. I would very much like to make sure you felt as good from an act of love that I preform on you as I did from the one you performed on me. Please, lay back and relax, enjoy the pleasures of ecstasy as they overwhelm your senses and render you hopelessly helpless to respond. I would feel so honored to make that happen for you, the way you made it happen for me." She started a sensual tongue massage on the protrusion of her upper lip and blew me a kiss, and I said, "You have no idea how much I would like to bury my face in your hairy pussy while giving it a cum-shampoo and pubic hair trim you will never forget. I have been making mental preparations for this process since the first sight ever I had of your fuzz patch snatch. You cannot imagine some of the things I have anticipated doing with your hairy home of flavored happiness. Maggie my dear, would you please honor me with the privilege of making unbelievable things happen inside the walls of my future want to be haven of happiness, your pussy parlor? I might even tie a pubic hair bow with my tongue and teeth around your super sensitive clitoris if you will allow me the time to do so. This act of lovemaking will require you only to lay back and relax, have as many drinks as you like and let me work miracles for you."

Maggie looked at me as though she was having a hard time believing anything I said and replied, "Pat, you sound like you are serious, but I really cannot tell. You are so different from any other man I have known it is confusing my comprehension. I want to believe everything you say, and still, your female opinionated verbiage carries only praise for the body and pussy occupation. You portray my armpit and the nape of my knee as having the same sexual status as my tits. You have given credence filled with curiosity and desire, for activities involving my anal opening to be considered with the same intensity and sensuality cries of ecstasy as do my vaginal pleasures." Maggie reached over to the nightstand and picked up the bottle of Southern Comfort. She appeared to be deep in thought while fixing her drink, then looked up at me with watery eyes and said, "My decision on truthfulness or bullshit is obviously not going to take place tonight, so I will answer you this way. As long as we are having fun and it feels good, and of course, the drinks last. Continue to explore and adore, that which you are so adamant about the consumption of. If it makes me feel good, like everything else you love to do to me, I am only left to implore, waltz me gently through this dance, but know this before you start, if you take me where I have never been, you are playing with my heart." Maggie then returned to her leaning back position and tearfully smiled at me, then quickly said, "Oh by the way, I will happily fix my own drinks. I do not wish to interfere with your upcoming performance or my beckoned pleasures. So, get started baby, I cannot wait. The anticipation of having a pubic hair clit bow is turning me on and pushing the restart button for all my motors."

That was totally unexpected, especially the part about me playing with her heart. Which is not something I really want to do. She put her heart on display, which gives me permission to play, with open consideration for heart conversation on another day.

My concentration was still in full bloom and flavored by the possible reception of rapture released through yielding to the temptation presented by her hairy home of clitoral happiness. With my tongue no more than a half inch from Maggie's clit, and my lips almost resting on the exterior of her pussy lips. All in the same move, I squeezed her buttocks with fingerprint power and forced loose lip pussy parlor to clit contact. Then for whatever reason I administered a bubbling vibration mouth to pussy lip rolling head bobbing blow-job to her cunt and surrounding fuzzy fenced in area. It delivered a thirty second continuous rumbling pussy fart that got Maggie's attention. She moved so quickly to sit up she spilled her drink on my head. The spillage began streaming down over my forehead and cheeks all around my mouth and into her love nest. Which added another interesting flavor for consumption. She exclaimed, "Oh my "God"!!!" "I have never done that before, what happened?" I figured I would let her think it was a malfunctioning body part for the time being, then try to explain it all later. I continued my quest to consume and partake of as much of Maggie's fur burger with as little interruption as possible. Besides, the mixed flavor of the draining Southern comfort with her love juices was pulling on my mind with strong enticement for consumption.

I never liked playing favorites while pleasuring a particular body part. I made it possible for me to treat her treasured fur burger fence line the same by beginning on my left, which would be the outside edge of her right pussy lip. I opened my mouth and with my teeth, lips, and tongue, I gathered a considerable number of pubic hairs for possible extraction. I gave them all a teasing tender tug to supply her love nest with the feeling of intrusion by minor pubic hair pulling pussy pain. Maggie responded with a little butt motion. Nothing serious enough to interfere with my mouthing process. Taking my time, I continued pursuing the circumference of her freshly Southern Comfort flavored snatch patch. Plucking with, and for the pleasure pubic hair pulling pussy pains would supply. I imagined a minor shock-like pain traveling ever-so deep into the walls of her pussy parlor, providing her with more pleasures as they were personally picked for plucking and circling closer together.

It seemed to be getting easier for me to single out and pluck an individual pubic hair. I was kind of happy about that because I had to choose from so many. To be able to maneuver my tongue well enough to single out one hair and position it between my teeth for the purpose of plucking, I considered quite a feat. On occasion I would allow myself the luxury of straying out into her fur burger wilderness and open my mouth wide while pulling Maggie's butt hard against my face and cover as much of her snatch patch as possible. Keeping my lips and teeth closed tightly together as I worked her buttocks with a rolling rotation. This procedure served as a pubic hair loosening process which almost allowed me to collect as many as I wished, by just closing my mouth. I could always count on having at least 10 or 15 to add to my little hideaway pocket for pincushion's. To say nothing of the tantalizing taunts of prickling pain to pleasure Maggie's twat. And pleasured she was. After I had worked my way about half of the way around her vaginal cavity, I stretched up to look and see how she was doing. She was almost lying flat with her head raised a little by the pillow. Maggie's eyes were closed. She was doing double duty with a rolling lip bite while performing an almost vicious massage on one tit. With the palm of the other hand Maggie was gently roll-crushing the other titty nipple onto overlay area. The lip bite would stop for a second and her tongue would come out and lick her lips to moist then returned to the bite role to continue. On her face was the look of ecstasy portrayed by frowning smiles while releasing moans of pleasure as she sucked her tummy in tight, so tight it almost forced my tongue from her twat.

After several serious attempts to give Maggie's clitoris a

bow tie, I made an adjustment to my attitude. I buried my ego in the midst of the most amazing flavor a Southern Comfort-ized scrumptious pussy could ever have, and just started munching out.

Maggie rewarded me again and again for my attentiveness to her scrumptiousness before the night was over. If blissfulness or orgasmic secretions were fattening, I would have probably gained 15 or 20 pounds that night. I do not know how long Maggie had been love starved before she met me. What I do know and found out in the coming days, weeks, months, yes, and even years, is that Maggie had an abundance of good love to give. I somehow had been blessed enough to have made her acquaintance and been the recipient of so much of her good love.

Maggie stayed on my schedule for quite some time. When she bought her own car, I gave her driving lessons on it. We would take road trips and go out of town for two or three days. Ounce we took a two-week vacation for a lovemaking getaway to Montego Bay and turned it into a very climatic sex on the beach holiday. The pearly white sand was sticking to every part of our bodies that had been blessed by the secretion of sex.

I always made myself available for Maggie's needs, whether they were additional driving lessons or lovemaking sessions. We kept the fires burning for about 2 ½ years at least once a month, sometimes more. I learned a lot from Maggie. One thing I learned was, we had a lot in common. Both of us had an insatiable appetite for the same thing, the art of making love, in every possible way one could imagine. I have no idea how she remained single, but then again, maybe that was the reason. Maybe Maggie could not find anyone to satisfy her or keep up with her and make her happy. What a shame, Maggie certainly deserved all the happiness life could bestow upon her, and she always worked hard for it. She loved to really put herself into and get involved in a lovemaking scene.

Maggie worked for the government and her job afforded her the possibility of being transferred to other countries from time to time. She accepted an opportunity to be transferred to France. We met one last time for a happy/sad lovemaking liaison. With tear filled eyes we presented each other with presents. One of the things she gave me was a monogrammed money clip I still have to this day. My most special present to Maggie was her personalized pincushion with my name on it. I had a seamstress put it all together for me. I had her stitch in white on the blue velvet material, to Maggie with love from Pat. Under that was, "As I promised your personal **("P-H")** pincushion"

We were both crying and laughing, but they were happy tears, for our final session of making real love and saying goodbye. Real love has a very special feeling. A feeling that lasts forever. I have that same feeling today as she revels the walls of my ***Wonderful World of Afterglow***. There, Maggie's memory honors me with her presence.

I never heard from Maggie again. I thought about her often and hoped she had found herself a French lover that could make her happy.

Chapter 10

"The 2 Student Boogie"

****

I was on my way to pick up Alyssa when I thought I had better stop and call the office. I tried to do that about every three hours just in case a change in the schedule would come up. Sure enough, there was a change in my schedule.

Alyssa had called and wanted to be picked up at a friend's house. The friend's house she wanted to be picked up at was also one of my students. Her name was Christine and she lived in Chantilly Virginia about 15 minutes from Alyssa. According to Alyssa, Christine referred her to me. I thought to myself, this could probably get interesting. Especially if Christine's husband was out of town, which happened quite often.

When I got to Christine's house, she and Alyssa were both standing outside. The garage door was open, and they appeared to be involved in a discussion about something inside. Either that or anxiously awaiting my arrival. I would like to think of course, that was the reason. I pulled in the driveway and they both came walking up to the driver side of my car. They gave me a very friendly reception and I was glad to see them as well. Especially, to see they were perfectly dressed for our driving lesson. They were both wearing shorts and a halter top. I turned the motor off and immediately inquired, "Do I have the honor of being blessed by the presence of you both for this evening's lesson?" Alyssa jumped in with, "Pat, get your country ass out of the car, I want to see those patent leather's." I looked at her, smiled and got out of the car then replied, "Your wish is my command my dear. Now can somebody please tell me what the hell is going on. Are we having a party, or, are we having a driving lesson?"

They looked at each other and then both looked at me and together in unison replied, "Both!" Then Alyssa said, "Unless you have something else, you'd rather do." I glanced at both of them. They were smiling and both providing a tender tap sliding caress the protrusion point of their upper lips with their tongues. I said, "There is no place I would rather be, and no-one I would rather be with than the two of you. So, which is first the driving lesson or the party?" Again, they both responded by saying, "Both!" I replied, "I have never tried that before, but I'm sure we can work something out with a little help from you young ladies." Christine chimed in with, "Well Patrick, I realize you do not have a preference and you were reserving this time frame for Alyssa, but I noticed there are several of my neighbors watching and I wonder if it would be okay for me to be the first to drive." Without looking around I replied, "I think that is a marvelous idea, Christine. Is it okay with you Alyssa?" Alyssa looked us both and nodded her head yes and said, "I will get in the backseat right behind you Mr. three-piece." And went around to the passenger side of the car, opened the door, and got in the back. Christine got into the driver seat and the duo's driving lesson began.

As we were leaving Christine's driveway I asked. "Where would you gorgeous young ladies like this lesson to take place?" Alyssa responded with, "I would like to see your apartment Pat. Christine said you showed it to her on her last lesson and I feel left out." Before I could say anything, I felt her hand coming around the right side of the seat. She dropped it in my lap and started moving it around to find the zipper in my pants. I glanced up at my mirror and could see Alyssa leaning forward looking over my shoulder. Then she asked. "I was wondering, Patrick, if you brought any cigars with you. I probably should not smoke it in the car, so I will just hold it in my hand if that is okay with you." That got Christine's attention and she said laughingly, "Smoke does not bother me honey, smoke it if you can get to it. I trust Pat as an instructor to keep us from having an accident while you swallow,

I mean inhale." Alyssa leaned up against the back of my seat and brought her left hand around that side of the seat to assist her right hand in unzipping my pants and unbuckling my belt. She loosened the waistband to my pants while at the same time giving my ear the rolling wet tongue teasing treatment. Christine was trying to check the scene out every couple seconds. That concerned me a little because she was a new driver. She realized Alyssa was having a little trouble hanging on to what she wanted to hold on to in order to complete her seductive, make believe, cigar smoking process. Alyssa was trying to wrap my cock up in both hands. Her arms were just a little too short to reach around the seat, so Christine very excitedly announced. "There is an abandoned section to this shopping center parking lot just up the street. Very seldom does anybody use that section. We could go there for privacy. Oh please, please Pat, can we go? I want to play too." They had both already pulled their halter tops down under their titty's, to supply the teasing temptation for my viewing pleasures while bringing me to an agreement.

I responded to Christie's plea by saying. "I am sure you are fully aware there is a driving school sign on this car which means that I am forced to act in a responsible manner, whether I wish to or not. I am trying to separate and measure the pleasures being presented to me by comparing them with my responsibilities, and how I should handle the situation. I have decided we will check out the parking lot for privacy possibilities. In other words, women are wonderful, and men are morons. I never argue with women, and I am always happy to exhibit my moron-ish mannerisms to bring them pleasure. If we get into trouble, we are all in it together."

Not only was I outnumbered, but I was totally open to any suggestion they might have that could possibly be considered party enhancing. Being unable to say no to a woman's desires always brought me pleasure.

The parking lot Christine had suggested was in fact unused with no activity. We stopped the car pretty much in the middle of the unused area. This way if anyone started to approach the car, they could be seen far enough away we would be able to make any body part adjustment necessary.

For the next several minutes Christine and Alyssa performed a magnificent molestation on my cock. Alyssa was eagerly applying an overzealous rapid-fire yank on my crank. While Christine was involved in a soothingly savage cum-slobbering suction-swallowing process. Between the two of them they succeeded in the total cum-saturation of the front of my pants, and we all had a lot of fun doing so. Including some back and forth, unusual comments such as, When Cristine was trying to supply Alyssa with a mouth, lip, and tongue transfer of my love lava. Alyssa pulled her head back and asked, "Christine, are you are fucking Dyke?" Apparently, she had tried to extract Alyssa's tongue. Christine replied, "I do not know for sure baby, but I am so damn hot to trot right now all I can think of is how much I would like to have my head so far up your ass I could lick your bellybutton from the inside." Alyssa started laughing, I had no idea what to think so I just said, "I sure as hell am glad, we took a few minutes to get to know each other. I think it is time for us to go to my apartment."

My apartment was about 15 to 20 minutes away in Annandale, Virginia. I insisted on driving. I knew I could deal with having my nuts busted a few times, better than I could with having one of them try to sit on my lap or suck my cock. After all, even though it was a driving lesson involving two of my former sex partners, in the long run I had to be concerned about the safest way to get there for all of us. I also knew I would have a lot of payback time to perform once we got to my apartment, but that was okay because I considered giving this kind of payback a personal privilege and pleasure. I was not sure if they were just joking with each other about their bodies or being serious, but I found out soon enough they both enjoyed the flavor of female as much as male.

We got out of the car started walking towards the building my apartment was in and encountered some pedestrian traffic. I insisted they both get in front of me to hide the wetness of my crotch area from people approaching us on the sidewalk. They thought it was funny and both tried to make sure they walked just the right distance apart so people could look between them and see what I was trying to hide.

When we got inside, I immediately took my jacket and vest off and laid them on the couch. They both grabbed hold of me and tried to assist in taking off my pants. While doing so, they hand gestured and rubbed the cum splattered area of my trousers. Rewarding me with interesting little tidbits of sexual innuendos. Once we were successful in shedding my trousers, Alyssa screamed out in a song like manner, "Where's the bathroom Patrick?" We found the bathroom and it took them about two seconds to bring each other to nakedness. They only had two garments and their halters were stretch-on. Naked were we all three in my shower, in Annandale Virginia. I remember like it was yesterday, Alyssa was a soap freak she broke her silence with, "Pat we only have one cake is soap in here. We need more. We all need one maybe two cakes apiece. Remember two of us have two openings to cleanse." I told them it was in the cabinet under this sink across the room from the shower. Christine volunteered to get it. As she performed her dainty little prance and bent over to open the cabinet, I had a mental memoir of her grass skirt and asked. Christine honey, why did you not bring your grass skirt?" She quickly replied, "I thought we would have enough going on, I did not believe we needed the grass skirts enhancement qualities." She returned with five bars of soap that she had already unwrapped. Which meant we had a bar for each hand. I figured if somebody did not try to stick one in my mouth, I would be fine. Alyssa chimed in with, "Patrick why don't you, fix us all a drink? Actually darlin' fix us a double, or just bring the bottle and a Coke for mixer. I know you have my favorite brand. I would hate to have to send you to the liquor store to pick it up if you don't. That would mean I would be forced to allow Christine to stick her head up my ass." as she laughed. I went to the bar got a bottle of Southern Comfort and a Coke but no glasses, classes in the shower might be too dangerous. I returned with the drinks to find Alyssa and Christine had their bodies locked together by a kiss and snatch patch finger-fucking. I took a double shot of Southern Comfort and chased it with Coke set the bottles down the corner of the shower and started jerking off, while enjoying the view as they pleasured each other's body. The excitement of watching them trying to pop each other's prune with a bar of soap from behind overwhelmed my desire to remain calm and cool while providing them lubrication for possible points of entry. Instead, it succeeded in energizing me with an early release of orgasmic bliss to reward them for what they were doing to my mind. Alyssa noticed I had busted a nut on the back of her leg and immediately broke their connection and dropped to her knees to drain my main vein. She had this fetish for cock sucking. I was blessed by a memory of our first rendezvous and reminded that anytime there was a cock on the loose she wanted it in her mouth. I immediately rewarded her with a déjà vu-ic eruption, that presented a "hole" interestingly different part for the three of us to play. The sudsing was underway. Within a matter of moments, we were all either sitting or in a semi-laying position, while suds surfing on the floor of the shower.

Alyssa had absolutely no problem taking the lead. And by doing so put her so far ahead of Christine and I, she started shouting out instructions. **Then Alyssa with a bar of soap in each hand, bega sudsing Christine's pussy and anal gland. While sucking my cock just like she had planned; She looked at Christine and said, "Make it last, follow me honey I'll get you there fast, start sudsing my pussy then favor my ass; when you have an abundance of suds to my lower arena, drop the soap on the floor and use your fingers for a reaming rim cleaner; Alyssa said to me with a smile on her face, "Patrick, I do not wish to tell you your place; but as a young man with such a desire to learn, keep searching for openings it is always your turn; if an armpit becomes idle you must favor it, you can always stay busy we both have two tits; you are a part of this company for more than just flair, the holes of our body we are willing to share; keep soap in your hands and love on your mind, and your place in this trio will be easy to find:"**

They were both kind of squatting in a covetous manner that made the body parts to be entered even more desirable. Alyssa suddenly broke the trend and grab my balls with both hands. She winked at Christine, then grabbed my shaft. They applied a very generous and thorough sudsing to my entire scrotum area. Then with a little tug from Alyssa, Christine turned her body and dropped to her knees with her face close floor. Alyssa stood up and bent over her with the bar of soap in her hand she used as a massaging dill-doe for both Christine's pussy and prune areas. My cock was covered with soap suds, Alyssa assumed the position and directed it into her anal opening. I received another memory from our first lovemaking session of her backdoor boogie love. ***She initiated masterful butt-body movement in a jack-off manner, as her ass hole whistled the Star-Spangled Banner; With slushing sounds of soap suds and desirable moan, from the pains of ecstasy as she backed up on my bone; Alyssa's ass swallowed my shaft again and again. While she fondled Christine in this trio of sin; adding fingers and prunes to this lovemaking art, Christine stole the show with a suds packing fart;***

I knew Alyssa had information I needed that could help me immensely in the future with my desired path of pursuit in the art of making love. There was something I was missing and needed to know about her desires for backdoor entry and oral sex. I also knew this was not the right time or place to pursue a conversation of that nature. I knew I would have to wait until we had our next driving lesson alone.

Over the next half hour to an hour, we used so much soap the suds were clinging to our bodies and the sides of the glass on the shower. I do not believe there was an opening, crack, or crevice, including between fingers and toes, armpits, nostrils, ears, and quite possibly mouths that had not been the recipient of the cleansing powers of a bar of soap. I can also confirm that soap suds change the flavor of love lava, and in my opinion the power of the pussy and the prune. I would much prefer to eat it with strawberry jam, honey, whipped cream, grape jelly, or Southern comfort, and most certainly, a mouthful of Dom Perignon would be a welcomed boost to the flavor of clitoral flooding. I never liked the taste of soap. However, this was an extremely enjoyable and very interesting little sidebar for sex that we had just been a part of. For that reason, I consider it a huge success and orgasmicly satisfying all around.

We were all, especially Christine and I, convinced that we had been thoroughly cleansed. Alyssa was the uncertain one. She seemed to be always in hot pursuit of a bar of soap and a crack or crevice to cleanse. This very simply meant Christine and I found our way to the bed first. We immediately joined forces and created a very sexually entertaining and awesomely appetizing version of that good "ole" Italian Taurus trait a (69'er). It was certainly my favorite and apparently one of Christine's as well. We had been eating each other silly by sucking and snorkeling the love juices our bodies were releasing. When suddenly I felt fingers crawl-caressing my ass crack in route to my anal opening. It was Alyssa, and in kind of a, I'm a gonna get ya voice. she said, "So, you couldn't wait for me - uuh."

Almost at the exact same time Christine and I broke our connection and asked, "You didn't bring any soap with you, did you?" Alyssa replied, "No, but I am about to lick my finger and let Patrick know just how much I appreciate him leaving me all alone in the shower of a strange home." Christine grabbed her hand and faster than fast placed it to her pussy and exclaimed! "Honey, you do not have to lick your finger, just gather up some of my pussy juices and it will make you feel so much better. Christine seemed very eager to help Alyssa make sure her fingers were reaching the inside of her pussy by applying a rotation movement to her butt as well as Alyssa's hand. The willingness they were both displaying for the partaking of pleasure from each other became obvious to me. It seemed Christine had found a fondling friend. Alyssa seemed very content to gather as much of Christine's love juices from inside her pussy parlor walls as possible. I began to think, and—there-- it was, the missing part to pull the three of us together. My cock was standing straight up and hard as a rock from Christine's mouthingly marvelous performance of tongue twirled magical molestation. I was in the right position I just had to move into Alyssa's line of vision. I had a feeling everything would just fall right into place. I moved my body a little just to make sure Alyssa could see what she needed to see. As soon as she saw it, she grabbed it with her free hand and my cock was immediately Alyssa's esophagus bound. I put one hand on the back of her head and my other hand on her tit. Then pulled her a little harder towards me while performing a one-handed titty massage technique that she had taught me on our previous encounter. Alyssa's body was now positioned perfectly for the upcoming performance of Christine. With the overzealous application of her other hand, Christine entered Alyssa's anal opening. It all started happening and the three of us became one.

For the remainder of the evening, we were body surfing and exchanging places. Bunghole bonding, clit clobbering, cum swallowing, pussy eating, cock sucking, butt fucking, armpit molesting, knee nap-ing, on occasion I would get lucky and be summoned in place to perform a titty fuck. While either Christine or Alyssa's finger found their way to my anal opening as they were performing mouth to pussy pleasures for the other.

When we finally started getting dressed it was about 9 o'clock. I asked Christine what time she needed to be home. She informed me there was no hurry her husband was out of town for two weeks and she was thinking about staying with Alyssa for a couple days. I suggested we stop and get something to eat on the way. I put on a different suit so I could eliminate the possibilities of a wet pair of pants.

When we were ready to go, they both suggested I drive. I always try to grant the wishes of young ladies, and I got into the driver's seat. Alyssa sat in the instructor seat, and Christine jumped in the back behind her. I asked Christine if she wanted to stop by her house to get a change of clothes. She informed me that would not be necessary. She said, "I will just wash what I have with me at night, and they will be dry for the next day." I guess that would not be much of a problem because she would only have to wash two pieces. I knew she was not wearing panties. I asked them if they had a preference of where they would like to go. Alyssa replied, "The Hickory Chick is not far from where I live. Since Christine is going to stay at my house tonight, why don't we just go there. Christine has never been to the Hickory Chick. If we go tonight, she will not fill like she has missed out on anything."

I was not really expecting that. I kind of thought they would have picked a restaurant or a carry-out. I think the way they were dressed had something to do with their desire to attract attention. Knowing the Hickory Chick was patronized largely by men where the attention would certainly serve as a mind-boggling ego builder. Their halters were charged with a cleavage disclosure and left nothing but nipple and overlay for the imagination. The shorts were skimpy also, barely covering their gorgeous little well-rounded bubbly bouncing butts. I had a feeling it was going to be an interesting time at the Hickory Chick with the way they were dressed. Especially as good as they looked. Hell, just thinking about it told me what I wanted to eat for dinner.

In a way I was kind of anxious to walk through the front door with these two gorgeous young ladies, wearing nothing but invitational memories, hanging on my arms. I wondered if Dwight or Richard would be there.

I was pretty sure they would be there and probably accompanied by their students. I opened the door to let the girls in first. As they walked through the foyer to enter the bar area of the restaurant, a cloud of silent interest fell on the Hickory Chick, and the "chicks" that caused it. They both turned to look at me and Alyssa quickly whispered, "Pat, you bring that sweet little country ass, three-piece suit patent leather shoes and all up here." With a little more hint of urgency in her voice, she quietly commanded, "Front and center, now!!!" As I stepped through the door of the bar entrance and moved forward between the two of them, it became increasingly clear that the attention level of the barroom occupants had been bestowed totally on Alyssa and Christine. Directly in front of the door entrance was the only booth that would seat more than four people. It was kind of a half-moon shaped booth with its back to the wall in the main window. Staring me in the eye was Dwight and Richard and their two lovely students. With a smile on his face Dwight said, "Parsons, bring your friends over here and introduce them. There is room in this booth for all of us." I walked over to the booth and introduced Alyssa first. She entered the booth then I slid in beside her and introduced Christine. She slid in on my other side. All eyes in the bar were on the two of them. Occasionally someone would look at me smile and shake their head. I started to put them both inside and set on the outside of the booth so they would not be so nakedly visible. After giving it some thought I decided the seating would be alright the way it was. Alyssa and Christine seemed to be enjoying the attention they were being given, why should I deprive them of their pleasure.

Once all the introductions were made and everybody began to feel a little more comfortable, all four of the girls decided they would go to the lady's room at the same time. I felt that was a pretty good idea and they might be safer that way. I offered Christine my jacket if she wanted it. She of course declined the offer, and Alyssa did as well. That made me feel like they thought they could handle whatever situation might occur whether it be a butt bite or an unusual comment.

Once they were out of sight on their way to the restroom, Dwight said to me. "Parsons, I got an ear full about you just a few minutes ago from the office for canceling all your students this afternoon. But from what I see of your situation right now, I damn sure don't blame you. I just hope you are learning a lot and I hope you do not get shot. As a matter of fact, it might be a good idea for you to pack up and go back home where you know you'll be safe." Richard jumped in with, "Yeah man, that might be a good idea. They say the husband around here all carry guns. Apparently, some of them have driving instructors names on them. My "ole" man always tells me, make sure you get the check at the first of the lesson and they are not married before you hit the sack. You probably should have stopped and bought a couple robes for them to wear in here. They might not be that safe in their present attire. You know some of these police officers get a little bit rowdy every now and then." I replied, "I asked them if they wanted to change clothes and they said no. I guess they figured if shorts and a halter was good enough for me to take them on a driving lesson it should be good enough to go to a bar in." Dwight said, "That depends on what kind of driving you are doing. And if you ask me, they knew what kind of driving they were going to be doing so that is why they dressed that way. Hey, do not misunderstand me, I like it. Hell, I wish they didn't have anything on." I came back to him with, "I'm sorry man, I didn't mean to cause any trouble, but on the other hand I do not think I want to pack up and go home. It is like that "ole" song goes, "I found a little piece of heaven here on earth" and I kind of like it." Richard came back with, "You mean you found a couple good little pieces of heaven." I smiled and said, "Yeah, hain't it nice, I like it here."

On their way back to our booth from the restroom the girls stopped and had a short conversation for two or three minutes at a couple different booths. The guys sitting where they stopped to talk were not in the company of young ladies. They probably gave out a couple phone numbers. Hey, if they were enjoying themselves, I did not care as long as they were safe and doing what they wanted to do. Dwight and Richard did not seem to be as content with that as I was.

When they got back to the booth, we had a few drinks and good conversation. Involving a few little comments with sexual overtones about showers and cleanliness being next to godliness. I think the girls brought up enough points about that to get the idea across so Dwight and Richard would understand we all had a little shower activity and cleansing process earlier that evening. Or maybe they were just trying to let them know what they had missed by not being their instructors.

After quite a few friendly, flirtatious sexually oriented introductions from bar occupants that stopped by the booth to say hello and invite them back, Christine and Alyssa decided it was time for them to go home. As they stood up and started to walk toward the exit they casually tugged and pulled their shorts and halter into place which drew quite an applause. Even some suggestions for an encore could be heard. I was not real sure what inspired it all until I talked to Dwight the next day. Apparently, Alyssa pulled her halter a little too far up and popped a nipple for a split second. She never mentioned it to me. I figured it was probably just her way of saying thanks for the attention and nice to have met you and oh by the way, here's a little something to remember me by, have a nipple.

When we arrived at Alyssa's apartment, I thought I would let them both out and go on to my place. But Alyssa had other ideas. When she realized I was not thinking of coming with them she said, "Patrick, don't you think it's a little late to be driving around alone with an unsecured heavy load? Find a parking place baby, we will wait here for you. We want you to come in so we can help lighten your load." I replied, "My dear young ladies, I am extremely greatful for the concern and desire you have for assisting me by sharing my load. *However, I have no intentions of leaving the two of you unbelievably desirable, tantalizingly teeth-marking mouth magnets, titillatingly tempting hunks of female flesh, standing here alone. This late at night dressed as you are, you would quickly become an all-you-can-eat take home care package.* You would be a very easy target. You must either come with me and we will walk back together, or I will wait here until you both enter the building. I will come up to your apartment after I park the car." Alyssa projected her dominance once again and replied, "Just what makes you think you would be safer than we would." And Christine came in with, "Patrick there are two of us." I replied, *"My lovely ladies, even if I were totally without clothes, naked as a jaybird running around in my suit of nature, I would be nowhere near as appetizing as either of you are. So, decide what the hell you are going to do. looking at you both standing there with nothing but making love on your minds is making me hungry. And thinking about you lightening my load is serving as foreplay to my mind and has warped my intelligence level to the point I have lost the desire or need for sleep. We shall have to substitute the sidewalk for a bed if you do not make up your mind pretty quick. I am suffering from malnutrition, and I need protein. I love to eat meat. So, what is it going to be?"* They both jumped back in the car. Christine was sitting partially on Alyssa's lap. She immediately pulled Alyssa's halter down and began a breast surfing process with her tongue from nipple to nipple. Alyssa laid one hand over in my crotch and the other one she stuck down in Christine's shorts searching out and massaging her ass crack.

After milling our way through a short session of unusually interesting sexual activities such as crotch pumping, tit sucking, finger pruning, and kissing. Yes, kissing plays a very important part in the art of making love. We all made our way back to Alyssa's apartment. I do not think it is necessary for me to convey to you that once in Alyssa's apartment I was treated like a king through the entire shower cleansing episode. I was told right from the start by Alyssa to sit back and enjoy the favors and flavors of their performance while they attended to my business. I will say, they took my business to pleasurable heights unknown, where they attended to it very well. ***The lightening of my load was underway, as the three of us prepared to share some bedtime play; It was like they thought it was my birthday, orgasmic bliss and love juice became their present of the day;*** I was the recipient, more so than they were. They were very serious about lightening my load. Alyssa said to me, almost like a line from a song, "It's your party Pat, cum when you want to!!!" It seemed like they were totally into getting me off. I think they wanted to see how many times they could bust my nuts.

It was definitely their playtime, and I was their toy. Alyssa lifted my head and put a pillow under it. Then granted me privilege by providing the pleasures of her treasure. She placed her recently shaven silky textured hairless pussy lips on my lips, and I made my request, **"BA-BY PLEASE, *SIT ON MY FACE AND MAKE YOURSELF HEAV-EN-LY HEA-V-Y!!!*"** Alyssa began a rock-a-bye pussy lip to mouth and tongue tumble move while Christine sprayed a circle of Cool Whip around the head of my cock. She began a cock sucking process that gave the term, "Cock Sucker," a whole new meaning. It was like my cock was receiving a vacuum cleaner suction with teeth stripping action on both up and down moves of my main vein. Christine knew how to apply perfect pressure without biting. It was a rigid stripping of my love juices. Alyssa and I were involved in a very sensual and soft sexual activity of her being orally gratified. Christine had lubricated her fingers and found the crevice between my ass cheeks. I was tongue twirling Alyssa's clitoris when she decided to penetrate my butthole with a two-knuckle finger deep insertion. I almost swallowed Alyssa's entire pussy parlor including her clit. She released a painful sound of ecstasy and begin to rotate her vaginal cavity fast and forceful. Her pussy lips were trail-spreading from inner thigh to inner thigh and all over her paradisaical parlor of pleasure. My tongue was stripping them of all the love juices they carried. Alyssa was having pussy muscle spasms from orgasmic bliss releases in a way I had never seen before. She pulled my head in hard and tight to her pussy while insisting on rough up and down, side to side and around rolling hard contact with my mouth teeth, lips, and tongue. The results were backfiring on her. She was lightening her load to extremes by cuming time after time with short little semi orgasmic blasts. Alyssa started to shiver and shake. I think this is something that happens to several ladies when they are going to experience an earthquake type orgasmic eruption. That is exactly what she did. Then she kind of leaned forward in a collapsing manner over my face which gave Christine a wide-open road for her other hand and as she deposited a rather fast finger butt-fuck to her prune, Alyssa screamed, "You mother fucking little cunt-licking butthole bonding dyke bitch, I'm going to get you for that one. You can bet your sweet little Hawaii grass skirt wearing ass-hole is going to be mine!!!" Christine started laughing and I dropped a motherload in her mouth, she choked and gagged. It drooled all over her chin onto the bed. I quickly said, "I hope you all are going to include me in these lesbian love liaisons which you are planning. You never know, I might be helpful to have around as an extra pole for penetration." Alyssa came back with, "Maybe another time, I'm still an amateur addict of lesbian love and not very good. Christine is my lesbian love nest instructor. This is something we had already planned to do after you went home. I hope you do not mind Patrick, nor do I want you to feel like you are being left out. But I am sure there will be another time if you so desire. We will set your curious little ass on fire with a lesbian love connection-erection. Hell Patrick, you never know it might give you a whole different outlook on the art of making love." I replied, "Hey baby, I already have a **"no hole's barred"** outlook on the way you two young ladies make any kind of love. You are from the Southland, and I am sure you are familiar with the line. "Nothing could be finer than dinner from your diners." I shall be waiting with bells on and a hard-on. With great anticipation for the partaking of any or all your newly acquired skills in the art of lesbian love that you wish to favor me with. Yes ma'am, I will be ready willing and able. It would be my pleasure to place my presence wishfully and willing to carry out your every command."

    I take great pleasure in letting you know the remainder of the evening belonged totally to my being sexually stimulated and ever so softly satisfied. It turned out to be the longest lasting, most enjoyable duetic love dance my body had ever been the recipient of to that point in my life. My every muscle, protrusion point, and orifices, were still tingling with memories of masterful molestation the next morning when I awoke. ***Even my fingernails and toenails were talking trash, and having sexual conversations with my eyebrow's hair and mustache;*** which oh by the way, was still carrying the remnants of the left-over love nests that had pleasured me by sitting on my face. ***My mustache blessed remnants of leftover love juices*** easily replaced the doughnuts to go with my coffee. My tongue is getting hard from the built-in desires of portrayal. I would still like to have a "doughnut hole" to soak it all up.

Chapter 11

Double duty/Double pleasure

****

I called my office next morning when I woke up. They told me I had a message that it was very important I meet with Dwight as soon as possible. They informed me that he had two tests back-to-back at the Arlington County DMV on Glebe Road.

I got ready as quickly as possible and headed for the Glebe Road Department of Motor Vehicles hoping I would catch him while he was still there doing road tests. Dwight's last test was just finishing up and he was waiting in his car for his student to come back out with their license. I walked over to his car and told him I had a message from the office to meet him there. He looked at me and started to laugh then said, "You must not have got much sleep, you still look and smell like last-nights leftovers." I came back with, "It was kind of early this morning when I got home. But a good time was had by all. They are good people and a lot of fun." He said, "Well, you are either one of the luckiest people in the world or the boss is playing favorites. You know the standard transmission car students are always the cream of the crop, and now you're going to have the American stick shift also." I asked, "What are you talking about?" He told me the office manager had left him a message this morning that they were going to turn over the American stick shift schedule to you in Virginia. He said he thought you could adapt to the switching of cars and combine the schedules easily enough.

He informed me that I could leave my car in the Hickory Chick parking lot. He said, "I will meet you there in a few minutes and we will drive to the dual control shop to pick up your car.

You have a brand-new car and a brand-new schedule plush your Volkswagen is also new, and you have only been working a couple months. It is a Rambler Ambassador, I guess they thought you needed a car the seats laid down in since you run around with all these women.

I am not sure how some of the instructors are going to look at this. You got two schedules and two brand-new cars, and I have personally seen you with more women than all the other instructors put together. I have a feeling that someone, namely an instructor, is probably going to say something." I replied, "The office manager told me they could not get instructors who wanted to teach the stick shift. I told him I did not mind teaching the stick shift, and that I had been driving stick vehicles all my life from the time I was five or six years old on the farm. And he told me that he would make sure that I got all the stick shift students in the state of Virginia. He also told me that it may be necessary as time goes by for me to help fill in on a stick shift schedule in Maryland and DC. I told him that would be fine with me."

The person that was under contract to put the dual controls in the car's name was Ron Knotts. It seemed like everyone called people by their last name, so we always referred to him as Knotts. He had known Dwight for several years and they were they were good friends. Over the years the more acquainted we got, Knotts became a friend of mine also. He looked at Dwight and said, "This is a really nice car for teaching driving. Who is going to be the instructor?"

Dwight looked at me and then back to Knotts and replied, "It will be Parsons's second car. The company is starting a new larger American car stick shift schedule. He Will be, hopefully, coordinating it with the Volkswagen schedule." Knotts looked over at me and said, "You must either know someone in the office or you made a good impression on them." I came back with, "Both I hope, my uncle is a distant relative to the owner and the office manager knows me pretty well. I used to be engaged to his niece. He asked me to come down and go to work teaching driving after his niece and I broke up. He is a good guy. He told me he would put me to work down here on the stick shift car in the state of Virginia, where 98% of your clientele will be young ladies between age of 16 and 35. And so far, he has kept his promise. Now I have to try to live up to what they expect of me." Dwight looked at me and said, "No damn wonder you got what you wanted. You were going to marry Willie's niece, hell Parsons, you were like family. Now I understand a little better why things are the way they are. Why in the hell didn't you tell me all this stuff?" I replied, "You never asked me, besides, even though it may be true, I did not want people thinking that I was getting preferred treatment because of a family acquaintance. I'm sorry man, I hope you understand that." Knotts kind of smiled and laughed a little and Dwight replied, "It ain't any big deal Parsons. We can still be friends and have a beer with some chicks at the Chick every now and then." I found out a little later that all the driving instructors referred to the Hickory Chick bar and grill as, the Chick. Knotts came in with, "All that other stuff is your business whether it's good or bad, but I can tell you this Rambler Ambassador is a damn nice car to teach on. The seats even lay all the way down." Dwight started laughing and said, "Knotts have you taken a good look at him? The only place he is going to get any sleep is probably in the car. That 98% female figure might be getting the best of him. If he were the right kind of friend, he would share." Knotts smiled a little, looked at me and said, "You got two brand-new cars and a good job. It sounds like the world is your oyster. All I can say is treat it right and do not turn it into an onion. Take care of your world, yourself, and your job. You might give Dwight some consideration every now and then if you feel he deserves it. After all, he is a friend and your boss."

    Dwight told me to drive the new car back to Hickory Chick and he'd meet me there in a few minutes and we go on a test drive for a training session. We both arrived at the Chick about the same time. He walked over to the driver's door and said, "You are the teacher, I will drive, and you make believe I'm a student. Expect me to respond like a student and be prepared for anything. This car has all the training accessories, you have a second steering wheel, a brake, gas pedal, and clutch. Do not hesitate to use them when it is necessary. I will let you drive some from that side also. And Parsons, do us both a favor, try to impress upon me the possibility that you know what in the hell you are doing. And you are going to be all right with this car and its schedule along with your other one. And if you would be so kind as to do it as quickly as possible, it would be appreciated. I am getting kind of thirsty, and I just heard a beer call ringing in my ear." I chuckled a little and told him, "Dwight, you know me well enough to know that I am not going to do anything stupid. I doubt if you have ever known anybody that thought more of himself and cared about his own safety as I do. And I believe you know you do not really have to perform this training program for me if you don't want to. As a matter of fact, if you do not, I will buy the beer tonight. He replied, "It's a deal man, let's go have a cold one and shoot the shit a while." And so it was.

I had been working the two schedules together for I guess two or maybe three weeks. I was fortunate enough to have the offices assistance in not overloading me with students so I would have time to make the adjustments necessary to coordinate the schedules. I had been privileged by the pleasures of having several lessons and sexual encounters with both Christine and Alyssa. Nothing had been said about the possibility of the lesbian oriented menage a trois they had mentioned. I was okay with that, I figured if they wanted to let me know and be a part of that performance, they would do that. I also had a couple rather lengthy wake up calls with Maggie during that period of time. Which was turning out to be a lengthy performance for appetite fulfillment on both parts. She was in love with the youthful twist I filled her lovemaking sessions with. I was in love with her sexual tenure and ability to transfer her skills to me. They complemented her lust filled longing for mouthful molestation of my cock extremely well. I fulfilled her youthful stud desire. Maggie was for sure one of the best, if not the best, cock sucker I ever met in my life. Her soft sexy, silky smooth, satisfying lip suction, still provide solace for my slumber.

Chapter 12

"My Blueberry Donut-Hole Lover"

****

As far as new arrival students for either schedule that had shown interest in not only taking driving lessons but the possibility of giving me additional sexual education

Pointers had not shown much promise. It was not like I was getting worried. I still had my old standby scheduled student/love makers that kept me pretty busy, and very happy. I guess it is that I like to bring in a new experience from the ages to the pages when possible. I somehow had the feeling that it would not be much longer before that event would occur. As it turned out I was right. I picked up a new student for driving lessons on the American Standard transmission car that lived in Falls Church, Virginia. She was 21 years old, and her name was Julie. Her appointment was for 8 PM and I arrived a couple minutes early. I thought if I got done early enough, I could stop by the Chick before everybody left. As the lesson progressed, she seemed inquisitively happy to find out, quite by accident, the seats would lay all the way down. It seems without letting me know she was going to attempt to adjust her seat while driving down Lee Highway. Julie pulled the seat adjusting handle a little too hard and suddenly disappeared. I laughingly asked if she was okay. She told me she was and was happy that I had dual controls. Maybe she did not realize it, but I was happy as well. As she was bringing her seat back to the proper position, she said. "That is a very convenient feature. What made you pick a car that the seats laid down in for a driver education car?" I replied, "I did not pick it, it was assigned to me by the office. However, I do agree with you, it is a very convenient feature. Especially if you are on a long trip or tired and you need to take a break and catch 40 winks." She looked at me without saying anything while portraying a smiling questionnaire. I think she knew by the way I received her smile, that was not the feature of convenience she had in mind. I said to her, "Julie let us pull into the next 7-11 we see. We will grab a cup of coffee and discuss the seats that lay down while setting up some future appointments for you." She agreed and asked if she could get two or three donut holes. I replied, "Sure, do you want to come in or shall I pick them up for you?" She said, "You can pick them up if you don't mind. I like blueberry glazed please." I said with a smile, "That's my favorite also, there not only good with coffee, but they are go good with anything you dip them in."

When I returned to the car with the coffee and donut holes Julie was nowhere in sight. My first thought was, where did she go. As I got closer to the car my question was answered. She had been trying out the feature of convenience by getting familiar with the seats laying all the way down. As Julie brought the seat and her body back to the normal position she said, I like the idea of the seats laying down they are kind of fun to play with. "You can hide from people if you do not want to be seen. I replied, "I like it also and I can tell it is going to have an interesting effect on teaching driving." By this time Julie was sitting up and her seat was secure. I handed her the coffee and put the donut holes on the dash. They came in a little clear plastic closed container. I said, "They are much better by the dozen. You have all that extra tasty smelling aroma closed in the container that kind of explodes and penetrates your nostrils when you open it. Blueberry donut holes have a special effect on me. That is why I bought a dozen so I would have enough of that blueberry sweetness aroma to accomplish its objective." As Julie opened the container, she took one out and touched it to her tongue. She began tongue surfing the ball shaped surface of the glazed doughnut hole and puckered her lips to take a bite, then said, "They turn me on." I could feel the sudden mental transferring of her tongue around my nut sack. The look on my face must have made it obvious, as she reached for another doughnut hole and said, "You'd better have one before I lick them all away from you. The flavor fills your mouth and satisfies your senses so much more intensely when you lick them all around like this." Once more Julie's mouth puckered caressing the blueberry flavored doughnut hole and with one bite it was gone. My groin area started sending sensations of nut popping vibrations. I grabbed a doughnut hole popped it in my mouth and said, "I am glad you enjoy them as much as I am enjoying watching you lick and swallow them. If you think I should, I will go back in and get another dozen." While mouthingly molesting and kiss caress swallowing another doughnut hole she replied, "That depends, Mr. Pat Parsons, on just how far you want this feeling to go and how long you would like it to last." That answered my question. Within a minute I came back with another container of donut holes. I was in such a hurry I ran by the cashier and had to go back to pay for them. By the time I returned she had eaten two more donut holes and drank a half a cup of coffee. I said, "Here you are Julie. I hope this will be enough blueberry flavored doughnut holes to allow the feeling to go as far as you want it to and last as long as you need." With another doughnut hole in her mouth she replied, "Teacher, I think I need some instruction on how to operate the seat adjustment handle." I was on it in a heartbeat. I took her hand in my hand leaned forward and over to her seat. I reached around to the seat adjustment handle and pulled. Julie was pushing her body back hard enough the seat immediately went all the way down and I went right along with it on top of her. She very quickly said, "Wow, that was fast, you are not only a good teacher, but you are smooth and fast with that seat adjuster button Patrick. Now I think you should instruct me on leaving this parking lot. We need to examine the flavors of blueberry donut holes together, while combining the experience and excitement of our favorite flavor with the feature of convenience. I know the perfect place for my seat adjuster buttons to be pushed. We would frequently end up there through the naughtiness of our night-time pleasures in my high school years." By lavishly licking and mouth molesting doughnut holes we helped each other control our mental desires as the novice Julie quickly drove us to a deserted dead-end street off Idlewood Road.

She was obviously much more familiar with the area than I. I had no idea where we were or how we got there. Julie's aggressive nature and charm had somewhat of a hypnotic effect on my haves and have-nots and had convinced me of what I should have. It was like the flavor and pleasures of watching her tongue licking that blueberry donut hole had stripped me of my responsibilities as a driving instructor. I was being dangerously neglectful to my world, as Knotts put it. Oh well, I can see how falling under the influence of too many lavishly licked, lip sucked, tongue traveled donut holes could affect a person's ability to think clearly. Julie was ready to go. She reached up got another doughnut hole put it in her mouth. Then she handed me one and said, "Come on Patrick, let's lay the seat down and share the remnants of two donut holes while we fall ponderingly victimized by each other's charms." And so it was.

Julie was abundantly blessed with charms but gave me very little time for pondering them individually. Instead, she flooded my vision, my thought processing, and my heart with all her charms at the same time. She may have been an inexperienced driver, but she knew how to get out of her clothes. She was totally naked before I could reach around and get the other front seat laid down. I was no longer in a pondering state of mind. No bra, no panties, what the hell was I going to do with this three-piece suit. She looked at me and smiled and asked, "Are you going to take your clothes off?" I reached her another doughnut hole and replied, "Yes ma'am I am, you may assist me in any way you wish. Right now, I like what I see, and I never get in a hurry when I am making love. The only thing I get in a hurry for is to cum. I shall try to be undressed by the time that happens. What I am looking at gives me the desire to provide your beautiful body with the bountiful blessings when I open the floodgates of the "Ole" Jizzem Trail." I took off my jacket, unbuttoned my vest and loosened my tie.

Then I began a kiss fondling procedure of her voluptuousness. As I started kiss skipping and nipple sucking from tit to tit, I spread her pussy lips with one hand and carefully bonded her doughnut hole with a blueberry glazed doughnut hole, then I asked, "Julie my dear lovely naked lady, would you indulge me in joining you and your lusciously lovely body of nakedness by removing my vest, unbuttoning my shirt, and taking off my tie." Julie knew what was about to happen, and she went a little crazy. It seems she was having a little trouble unbuttoning my shirt, so she just ripped it off stripping the buttons. That was fine with me, I didn't like that shirt anyway. Shirts have no business interfering with sexual pleasures. I was right where I wanted to be. In my mouth I had two donut holes releasing excellent flavor with aromatically seductive qualities exploring my nostrils.

Since it was my first attempt at making love in the backseat of this car, I had to make several experimental body moves to find out how much room I had. Making sure to keep my mouth and lips and tongue securely planted on the entrance of Julie's vaginal parlor of pleasure, I busied myself treasure hunting for her blueberry flavored clitoris. Then while devouring the mixed flavored edible remains of her pussy pleasantries, I casually lifted my butt up and rolled the lower part of my body over on the other laid down seat.

With a slight bend in my knees, I was able to get in partial position to preform my favorite pleasures.

Julie was starting to get a little frustrated from not having anything to play with or put in her mouth. I got her another doughnut hole and as I touched it to her lips, she pushed her head forward and tried to swallow my fingers and bit them slightly when I was pulling them out of her mouth. I began a rough rolling circular tongue massage on her clitoris which quickly produced a couple mini blasts of dripping love juices. She immediately began a very viciously vigorous tongue fucking process by slap-slamming my mouth hard with her snatch. Julie was not bashful in letting me know she was hot to trot. Along with my hard pressing clitoral suction it only took 10 or maybe 15 pussy power plunges to produce a volcanic eruption of love juices. Saturating the remaining parts of the blueberry donut holes which increased the pleasures of consumption. It was almost too sweet to eat. I became artistically inclined, and pleasure painted pictures with my tongue. Rolling her love lava around the inner walls of her pussy parlor and savoring the flavor in my mouth before satisfying my desires to swallow.

Julie was releasing whimpering screams of ecstasy and squirming her body around trying to rub up against my legs. Although I hated to do so, I broke my mouth to pussy connection so I could unbuckle my pants and pull them down below my knees. As soon as that was accomplished, Julie grabbed my cock and pulled herself into position to ride topside of a (69'er). Although her esophagus was not as pronounced as some others may be, my cock had been patiently waiting for some Julie's E train travel. It had been imprisoned behind the zipper and a pair of pants while suffering from hidden hardness. No sooner did the head of my cock touch the first rib of Julie's esophagus than the floodgates of the "Ole" Jizzem Trail flew open. I dropped a mother-load in Julie's throat and flooded her E train rib cage. She choked and gagged two or three times but tried hard not to lose her long-awaited mouthful of love juice.

I continued to ride that train and made sure her excrement harvest was abundant so she would have plenty to mix with the remnants of her blueberry donut holes. Julie supplied me with short little mini blasts of clitoral weeping climax's for at least a half hour. I suddenly got the urge to have more room to work out a pleasurable presentation for Julie's first ride and I said, "Julie, I am glad we were able to work it out so you could experience the feature of convenience for the first time with me. I only live about 10 minutes from here. I have a king size bed, hot and cold running water, and I serve drinks with sex. I would very much like to pleasure your treasure in the comforts of that environment if you would allow me to do so. I hope you do not misunderstand; this was fun, and I have enjoyed it immensely. I could treat you so much better with more room to operate. And that for me is what it is all about. I like to make my partners happy. I want you to be happier when it is over than you were before it started. That being said, should you choose to stay in the confines of this semi backseat bed, I shall endeavor to provide you with all the pleasure I can muster, and as many overflowing orgasms as time and our bodies will allow." She nibbled nipped the head of my cock three or four times and slobberingly mumbled, "I want to go to your place." We quickly got dressed enough to travel and I drove. *Julie found room in my lap to put her face, until we reached our destination she kept my prick in place; As we hurried to get inside I fumbled for the key, she quickly let me know she wanted more of me; while undressing once again my mind it did concur, there was no doubt about it I needed more of her; we were fucking and sucking in the comforts of a shower, Julie was like a hungry nymph as she released her pussy power; and as I prepared her gift with my prick just like a rock, bouncing off the walls to find a hole to hide my cock; somehow we got involved in a sexual wrestling match, Julie swallowed all my meat while I devoured her snatch; time was unimportant still we had none to waste, all wrapped up in towels we were starving for a taste; I put my arms around her waist and turned her buttocks up, with my face between her thighs my tongue was in her loving cup; as my hands pulled on her shoulders her lips molested my cocks head, she performed starvation suction until it started to turn red; we did everything in unison my hands pulled as her thighs squeezed, we tried to paint a perfect picture so we could both be pleased; I performed a sexual ballet bounce with our bodies round the room, with full awareness that from bouncing the more of each we could consume; we were like two starving animals that had not been fed, enough would never be enough and we still had to play the bed; like her starving little pussy Julie swallowed blast after blast, I had the happy to be hungries for she was cuming fast, I pulled up hard on her shoulders and my tongue tickle tipped her clit, she did a double squeeze with her thighs that begged me not to quit; we were salivating in loves juices as we waltzed across the room, I pulled a slippery nose slide and tickle tongued her pretty prune; she went a little crazy I guess bananas is the word, if I had one in my hand an unknown language would be heard; Instead I chose to use a handy tool and plugged her with my thumb, with full first knuckle deep insertion Julie dropped a double CUM; We found so many different ways to set our body fluids free, we both worked hard at pleasing like it was meant to be; although we had only met today we knew each other oh so well, to pleasure one another was like the ringing of a bell; I continued with my quest to bring her more orgasmic bliss, she found a way to make sure a busted nut I would not miss; to ride the E train upside down would be a new one for the books, I thrust my shaft up in her throat until her body shook; she smacked my ass and bit my prick and began a savage suck, I jammed my cock into her throat and her esophagus I did fuck; she squeezed her thighs to give my nose a surprise as her pussy did explode, my nostrils filled with her love juices when Julie shot a mother-load; through our persistence we both pleasured by stepping love up one more notch, our hunger was addictive as we feasted on each other's crotch; both filled with monomania for the desire to make love finer, the bed was so inviting it brought closure to our stand-up "69"er:"*

I stepped backward to the bed and sat down on the edge. I wanted to keep things going. I held everything in place and tried hard not to stop. Julie broke her cock connection and said, "Lay back and spread your legs. Baby, you have been so good to me, I just want to suck your cock for three days straight with no breaks." I thought it was a little strange that she would say 3 days, instead of 1day, or 1 week, or 1 year. "I asked her, "Why 3 days, don't you think that is a bit of a lengthy process for a continuous blow-job?" Julia replied, "That is when my next lesson is scheduled, and I just might suck it three more after that." I had no objections, so I scooted around into a spread-eagle position on the bed and said, "That has never happened before. I am always into trying something new, but I don't know if there will be anything left after three days for you to continue to suck." Julie still had my prick in her hand, giving it soft smooth little jerks and responded with, "You just leave that to me Patrick. I will make sure there is something still left for me to suck on." Once we got into position she went straight back to work. She was a fantastic cock molester. She said, "Put your head up on the pillow, I know you must be tired. I just want to bring you pleasure like you did for me. I will suck your cock until my lips and numb and then I'll jerk you off. I want all the cum you have baby." She was telling the truth. She would suck and swallow for a while, then wrap her fingers around my cock and begin a five-finger rapid-fire masturbation process. Julie could tell when I was getting ready to cum and put her face right in front of the head of my cock. When my nuts busted, she sprayed it on her forehead and rubbed it through her hair. Then sprayed her cheeks and rubbed it around her body to her tits and into her pussy. She brought her hand back to her mouth and performed an individual finger vacuum molestation. Julie provided a sultry sensual secretion suck off process on each finger. She also allowed each one to do an individual finger tap dance thank you, on the protrusion point of her upper lip and said, "Pat you have such sweet flavored cum, you must have eaten two or three honey sandwiches last night." Then Julie wrapped her soft service minded vacuum cleaner cock sucker lips around my shaft and began a sucking search for all the love juices I might be trying to hide in my cum compartment. I was not trying to hide anything. From what I had learned about Julie in this short period of time, my cum would be the last thing I would try to hide. Hell, Julie not only wanted all the cum I could possibly provide her with, but she knew where it came from, how to inspire a cum arrival, and how to get it out to where she could put it in her mouth and swallow. Julie had a true **cum addiction.** She enjoyed cum in her hair, in her armpits, all over her body, around her tits and in her bellybutton. Julie had an insatiable cum appetite for every bodily orifice she possessed. I think the only time she would be happy or halfway satisfied about it, would be if they were all filled with cum and running over. While lying there thinking about all this cum and her body,

I wondered if she ever had a **"cum-body-massage"**. Suddenly that gave me an idea for the next part I might play in this, what is turning out to be, a very involved lovemaking session/driving lesson.

Julie's suction cup fetish for the head of my cock, continued for at least another hour or hour and a half, maybe two hours. After all, my mind has never been equipped with the mental mode for clock monitoring.

I was trying to catch a wink every now and then. Julie was totally in tune with what I was thinking. About the time I started to snooze she would stick her finger in her pussy for a fresh juicing and lubricate my anal opening. Julie provided me with an eye-opening Introduction that consisted of her middle finger driving a double-knuckle deep insertion into my ass-hole. Which was, without a doubt, one of the rudest awakenings I ever received. I suppose she considered it a part of her driving lesson.

After the reoccurring of that particular process, I decided not to try to go to sleep anymore. Hell, I was afraid to even close my eyes. Julie was enjoying this too much. She had told me she wanted to pleasure me, but I was beginning to get a little concerned about the length of her fingernails bringing me more discomfort than I really felt like putting up with. Consequently, I made a suggestion that included something I knew she would like. It required us switching places and her spreading eagle. I was straddling her like a saddle over her tummy on my knees, swinging my balls to and fro and around. Dropping them down for a dragging tiptoe over her two lips from time to time. I enlightened her as to my intentions of presenting her body with a massage she would never forget. I said, *"**Julia my dear, my lovely lady of the night, you have brought me much pleasure, now 'tis my desire to make things right, I shall bring you a double measure, with a fast blast of hormonic delight**.* You say you want all the cum I can give. I am going to be your personal masseuse and cum all over your body. Then, with tender loving care, **I shall rub in your cum-toddy."**

Julie responded by grabbing my cock and surprising me with an application of quadruple suction and a short shot of thumb to prune bonding. I am not sure what to think about that. It is not something I am crazy about, and I did not have to worry about it all the time back home. But in this area, every lady I have been with always shows a serious interest for prune bonding. I suppose it is something I shall have to learn to deal with, and not allow myself to develop the flavorful addiction this area appears to be contaminated by.

I slid back and took my prick away from her. Bent down and gave her a long salivating love juice stirring kiss. As we broke our kiss connection, I decided to dip into a little prick to pussy pounding with10 to 15 rapid-fire, force filled strokes of motor muscle fucking. Identifying me as an automatic dispenser of cum juice. Julie's internal combustion chamber produced a clitoral explosion that provided me with the desire to occupy her pussy parlor a little longer. I gave her two or three short kisses around and about her nose, cheeks, and mouth, then slowly put my butt in reverse while reamingly backing out of her love nest. With my cock in hand, I slowly stroked it while returning to my knees and ball dragging position. The stroking process produced several little dribble-drops of her favorite flavored body juices. I looked at her and said, "I know you want to play Julie, but allow me to play my prick for you while I cover your gorgeously edible, scrumptiously sexy body with cum. Lay back my dear Julie, rest your mind and your body while allowing my energy to control your senses and supply your sexual desires." I stretched up to give her a kiss and realized she had started finger fucking herself. I smiled at her and said, "That looks so nice and sexy, and I am sure it will enhance my serving you with cum droppings to mix with your sexual secretions of love for finger lubrication. Damn Julie, you are a sex hungry little bitch. You are a sex pot and I like it, go on, finger fuck yourself while I watch and stroke. It will serve as an enticement for me to provide you with a double dose of cum droppings. Under the circumstances I was not about to try to stop her from the pleasures of self-masturbation.

Quite the contrary, I was happily and hungrily encouraging her to do more and go faster with her self-finger pleasuring performance. Every single move of her body was inspiring me to work harder and move faster to fulfill my desires to cover her body with cum. She ran her fingers through her hair, I pounded my prick faster. She opened her mouth and started sucking her finger. My prick was pulsating with reckless endangerment on its mind for a flood of cum. Julie saw me moving faster, she began to squirm and push her pussy up to meet her finger. The collective scene of her lips finger caressing and a shimmy shaking butt bounce finger fucking as her pussy swallowed the middle digit of her hand, caused the floodgates of the "ole" Jizzem Trail to blow its doors off and covered her face neck and tits with a backed-up overload of love juices, or **CUM**, as she prefers. And right now, it is all about what Julia prefers.

She immediately went to work with her other hand rubbing it all over her, through her hair and around her body. Realizing this was now a team effort, I took my other hand and assisted her with an armpit and titty massage. Julie kept on pounding her pussy with her finger and I kept on pounding my prick with my hand. The temptingly tantalizing sexy site of my action to her and her action to me, succeeded in bringing forth another explosion. Julie gave one long strong surge upward and busted out bawling. Loving her body with my eyes had inspired me to bring her even more pleasure by making another trip to my storage compartment of cum. Julie's butt was bouncing up and down on the bed like she had a spring-loaded apparatus in her ass to make it go up and down. I visually made love to her as long as I could. Then I blew them damn gates off once again, this time covering her middle torso and filling her bellybutton. I immediately pulled her hand away from her pussy and smotheringly rolled her clit with my cock. Julie showed her appreciation by trying to fill the hole in the head of my prick with her clitoral seepage. I drove my shaft hard against her pussy walls and started a reaming process. She began to cry and started screaming yes-yes-yes, deeper- deeper-deeper, oh yes fuck-me, fuck-me. She viciously slapped my back with both hands and dug her fingernails in. I could feel them scraping down over each rib on the sides of my back. I immediately dropped down and gave her a kiss, then we started tongue swallowing and body surfing.

This was not exactly what I had in mind when I said I was going to give her body massage, it was so much better. We were performing in rhythm a grinding-slide to explore the low and high points of our bodies while moving with togetherness rubbing the juices in. Julie started smacking my ass and I started pounding her pussy harder and dropped another load. We ravishingly reveled in and with each other's bodies and love juices until falling asleep in the sticky witness of love's charm and each other's arms.

The next day I took a break in my schedule and gave her a call to see how she was feeling and if she was ready for me to drop by to pick her up and take her home. I have no idea why, but I am glad I did. She informed me that she was still at my apartment wallowing in the wonders of last night's love. She had called in sick and told them she did not know just how long she would be off. Then She said, "I will be here when you get home. I am making mental preparations for a repeat performance. If you want anything to eat you better have a bite before you get here. I shall be dining on your cum filled love muscle and sexy body. I hope I can supply you with many nutritional overloads as well. Hurry home baby and bring me your rock-hard cock filled with cum."

The information I received in that conversation seemed to be much more welcome than I could imagine it being. Later I understood why. This young lady and I spent 11 ½ years together. Those years filled, to the very last day, with the same flavor for loves specialties as described previously on the pages of this book. We were engaged and came very close to marriage several times. **She was my Queen!!! She still holds "Queen Status" in my wonderful world of Afterglow. As I fumbled through the cobwebs in the corners of my memory filled mind, to the time when we were together, I realize just how much "GOD" has blessed me. I thank "GOD" every day for the wonders of youth, both mentally and physically, for the power of perseverance and** potency possessed by those who have only to look forward to their Wonderful World of

"Afterglow."
{6/26/76 TO 10/10/87}

I have become very familiar with some good "ole" country song titles that someone like myself just naturally thinks they were written for him. Johnny Cash George Jones and Hank Williams Sr. had a way of making you think that.

*There was Johnny with,- "**I Still Miss Someone**"!*
*And there was George with,-"**I'll Be Over Her When The grass grows over me**"!*
*And there was Hank with,-"**I'm So Lonesome I Could Cry**"*
These guys could kill you with heartache if you let them. Somehow it never seemed to work that way for me. They always just brought back those beautiful memories that now hold up the walls of my wonderful world of **"Afterglow."**

I wish you all the best.
but as "Ole" George Jones once said,
"There's Nothing Better, Once You've Had The Best"
So with words of wisdom from the Midnight Mumbler

**I say no more
and shut the door!!!**

Chapter 13

Fraulein fever

****

It was about 8 o'clock on a quiet Sunday morning when I got to my first student's house in Falls Church, Virginia. She lived in apartment's right off Broad Street. Her name was Sabrina, and she was from Germany. She had been in this country about a year and a half and had a 14-year-old daughter. I got this information from her on our first lesson just a few minutes after we started. I always tried to get a conversation going to help the student relax and calm their nerves. Especially the older ones, like Sabrina.

I found out when I was taking her information down that she was 31 years old. She seemed a little more nervous than the average student her age, so I made sure to try to keep the conversation as normal and low keyed as possible. Apparently, she had become a mother at a young age. I wondered about it, but I did not breach the subject. She eventually got around to telling me about that situation as well as other points of interest in her life while living in Germany. She included a few little tidbits of near to nothing information on happenings after she arrived in the US. After about two weeks and five or six lessons we had progressed to a level of almost best friends. I knew pretty much everything about her, and she knew pretty much everything about me that could be discussed in normal conversation. She worked in a local convenience store that sold German food and carry out sandwiches. Her daughter went to Madeira school, which was a private girl's school. She already knew how to drive an automatic and had a Virginia driver license. She wanted to learn to drive the standard transmission before her daughter became of age to drive so she could teach her to drive a stick shift car. I gave her my ideas on that, which were, she might think about providing her daughter with the basic fundamentals of stick shift driving. With traffic being the way it is today she needed to get professional driving lessons with dual controlled automobiles and a licensed professional driving instructor.

I had scheduled Sabrina for my last student of the evening. Hoping I might be able to be of assistance in unlocking her door for her when the lesson was over. Which of course would mean it would open a door for me to become a more versatile driving instructor friend. Since her daughter lived at school during the week and came home on weekends, it presented an almost perfect situation. I suggested she pull in a parking lot, and we could practice parking a couple times before her lesson ended. Naturally, quite by accident, I picked a parking lot with a restaurant that had a private bar section away from the regular dining area. We had parked a couple times and I said, "Sabrina you have done such a good job driving and parking tonight I feel your need for my instruction very fast coming to an end. I think I would like to buy you a drink and toast to your perfection as a stick shift driving student and our friendship, shall we. Sabrina smiled and without hesitation replied," I would like that, but I am going to keep you around as long as it takes for me to feel really comfortable driving a standard transmission car. And that just might turn out to be longer than you think." I said, "That will be fine, I want you to be comfortable, and it gives us more time to build our friendship. We might as well start doing that right now. I promise to be at your beckoned call for as many driving lessons as you think you need. After all, you are a young lady with a Virginia driver license, and that makes you the boss. The truth is my dear, the young lady part is what makes you the boss."

As we walked into the bar area, I spotted a booth that was a little farther away from the bar area than the others. I asked her if that would be okay with her. Sabrina replied, "Yes that's fine, it seems like it is a little more private also." I wanted it because I knew they were going to ask for my ID, and I of course wanted to be as far away from everybody else as possible. I had it ready so they could check it quickly and quietly and it would be over. I guess Sabrina noticed I was a little out of sorts because of the ID check and she said with a smile, "Wait a few years and you will pay them to check your ID." And I honestly can remember a few years back, giving somebody a pretty fair tip, just because they asked me for my identification when it was so obvious that I looked old enough not to be carded. The carding business gave Sabrina an opportunity to tell me she did not think I was egotistically sensitive enough to let something like that bother me. It provided a little conversation topic if nothing else.

I asked her what she wanted to drink, she informed me that she knew they did not have what she liked so she would have what I was having. I of course was having a Southern comfort mixed drink and I said, "This is a nice smooth drink however, you must be careful. It is high in alcohol content with a sweet flavor." She replied, I am glad you told me, but I like my drinks kind of strong. I have my favorite at the house. You will have to try it sometime. It is made in Germany and very hard to get over here. I bring a few bottles with me when I come back from a visit." I asked, "What is the name, maybe they have it." She told me the name and said, "Don't bother asking, I would just have to spell it for them. I am fine trying the Southern comfort."

We both seemed a little thirsty and took care of our first drink rather quickly. By the time we had a couple more the conversation was beginning to get interestingly flirtatious. Sabrina made it quite easy for me to be aware of her playful intentions. Almost every time we spoke, she would either lean in toward me or rub her leg against mine. Clearly giving signs of someone in need of touch. I responded to her needs in a timely manner staying in tune with her lead performance. The conversation was getting to the point where all the questions were being asked by the eyes and answered the same way. With minor touchy-feely in the booth, our minds eyes were visually making love. I decided to take a chance and leaned over and whispered, "It is getting kind of crowded in here. Do you have an extra bottle of your favorite drink that we could share?" During the whispering process I presented her ear with tender little teasing nibble nips accompanied by a slow licking blow-job. Sabrina quickly responded by squeezing my hand and saying, "Why don't we do that?" She revealed the evening's outcome with a certain delightful look of no-nonsense on her face. She knew where we were going and what we were going there for. I think she felt the same as I about taking our friendship to the next level. I called the waitress over and asked for check. By the time she returned with our check the body talk had progressed to being a little too busy for that isolated booth to remain unnoticed. The waitress cleared her throat to let us know she was back and ready to take payment for our check. I paid the check, and we made our exit, raising a few eyebrows along the way. We had taken about two steps outside the back door entrance to the restaurant where the parking lot was when Sabrina turned and looked at me. We both knew it was time to give a long overdue lip lock performance with tongue extraction capabilities. Sabrina was trying to climb one side of my body as far up as she could in a thigh and calf molesting manner. By the time we got into the car it was obvious something had to happen. Once again, the eyes asked the question, and delivered the answer. Neither of us said a word as I reached over for the button and laid the seat down on her side. Sabrina had started a slow dry jacking move on my cock from the outside of my pants. Needless to say, it happened right there on the restaurant parking lot. We were in a driver education car with signs on it and seats that laid down. Thank "God" for the ingenuity of the rambler ambassador's car manufacturer. Sabrina unzipped my pants as I laid down. It was so obvious on both our behalf's that we had been devouring each other with our minds, and our first sexual encounter had to be a ("69"er). Our prior mental preparation and body moves from that little isolated booth was in total agreement on having a body feast. I do not know what words Sabrina used to describe her mental desires. But I had developed a hunger for this very attractive German lady's love juices on our first Sunday mornings lesson. There was nothing on my mind except going down to get a mouthful of her pussy and favoring her clitoris with some tender tongue molesting moves. That thought always made me think of a song that fits the situation. I first heard it when I was in high school. The first few lines went like this, *"I got a brand-new car and a tank full of gas a mouth full of pussy and a handful of ass, come and tie my pecker to a pole to a pole, come and tie my pecker to a pole, I wouldn't use it though it's hard like a rock, I'm going to eat her pussy and she can suck my cock, just tie my pecker to a pole to a pole, just tie my pecker to a pole.*

Pardon the interruption, now back to partaking of some sweet German pussy juices. Sabrina quickly laid claim to the topside and started to gobble. I pulled her dress up over my head and her panties down below her knees. She spread her legs as wide as she could, and I shoved my face into her snatch. With both hands on her ass, I pulled her pussy down hard to my mouth. My tongue immediately presented her clitoris with a love song of tender twirling suction, and I became the recipient of my first taste of German love. Her sweet flavor filled pussy juices came in three or four different little squirts. I had already blessed her tonsils with a couple busted nuts. I think I busted the first one before she got my cock halfway in her mouth. I guess it comes from premature youthful desires of being eager to please.

We both ate our fill, which took quite a while. It certainly could not have been considered a quickie. Sabrina had such flavorful pussy juices and soft cunt lips. I could have eaten her until she became a missing person if it had not been that her dress was slightly restricting my breathing.

A fully clad ("69"er), we had not even taken off our shoes. I do not know about Sabrina, but that was another first for me. The nice part about it was all we had to do was pull the seats and our clothes up, then drive four blocks to her apartment.

I had been taking my favorite trip through her tubular tunnel of esophagus love, trying to flood the entrance by filling her throat and floating her tonsils with love juice. We were both overwhelmed by each other's constant cuming. We had spent the entire time swallowing mini blasts of orgasmic bliss from clitoral explosions or the dribbling drool of a busted nut. My desire to have Sabrina's lips surround my cock and massaging my balls as she presented me with a ticket to ride her E train began when we first met. I have heard lots of guys talk about the tits and ass. I have always been an eye, lips, and esophagus man, when it came to determining whether I thought a lady was going to be a miracle worker at the art of making love. Sabrina talked with a slight German accent. The way she formed her mouth and moved her lips, jaws, and head when she was speaking, not only got my attention, but it turned her esophagus into a portrait of inviting appeal.

My long-awaited dream of desires had come true and produced an out of control, number of busted nuts. I was not even given the chance to confer with the floodgate keeper of the "Ole" Jizzem Trail. She had taken total control of that process and was somehow able to enjoy a constant delivery of my cum droplets.

Sabrina was kiss caressing my cock and balls as she slowly terminated my ticket to ride with a soft slobbering lip squeeze and tongue rimming. She very appreciatively tucked them away and zipped up my pants. I sensually tongue gestured and nibble-nipped both of her butt cheeks and gave her inner pussy lips a gentle tongue-rubbing massage. I collected her leftover German love juices with my fingers and lubricated her ass crack while tongue twirling her prune. Then replaced her panties and kissed her pussy and both ass cheeks again. I wanted to make sure they knew I enjoyed their company and was planning on a repeat performance soon. Sabrina had flinched a little when I twirled her prune. That left my thoughts in limbo for it being a future sexual avenue. Which was fine with me, I was not crazy about it myself.

I was really beginning to enjoy my training program for sexual encounters. One thing I have always been curious about, is how so many women could produce the same results in so many, different ways. I guess it is just another one of those double **W's. Women Are Truly Wonderful!!!**

As we were walking from the car to her apartment building, I noticed Sabrina seemed to be in somewhat of a hurry. I did not think much about it at the time. After we got inside and was approaching her apartment door, she started searching through her purse for the key. I quickly put my hand on her hand and said, "Sabrina, you have worked so many miracles in my dream world tonight, I wonder if I could ask for one more?" She looked at me and smiled, then with her German accent replied, "Sure, if I can, I will do it." My prick immediately responded to her mouth and facial movement by a stiff standup salute to her esophagus. I said, "Earlier today I had a daydream that I was helping you unlock your apartment door. Would you make that dream come true by allowing me the privilege of unlocking your door?" She twisted her head a little sideways and handed me the keys, and said, "It is alright." Another blast of sensual sensation was knocking on my zippers door as I unlocked hers.

Once inside her apartment she made it obvious why she seemed to be in such a hurry to get inside. The only thing she appeared to be interested in doing was making sure I enjoyed her favorite drink as soon as possible. She got two glasses and poured us both a drink. Then Sabrina proposed a toast to all cars with seats that laid down. We both emptied our glass and I said, "Wow, no wonder you like it so much, that is really good. Could I please have another? I have a toast to give also." She poured us both another drink and I stepped back to allow my eyes the pleasure of visually devouring her body. While doing so, I gifted her with a couple short nibble nipping massage moves of soft rubbing my lips with my teeth and tongue as I paid special attention to her eyes, lips, and esophagus. Without giving it a second thought, she sat her drink on the table, then took mine did the same and said, "You can make later."

Sabrina knew she was the boss and totally aware of the powers of the pussy. She knew exactly what she wanted, where to go and how to get it. She attacked me with another leg climbing tongue extracting kiss and began unbuttoning buttons and loosening my tie. This was her way of showing me around the apartment. When we finally got to the bed we were totally undressed. Sabrina flipped on the nightstand light, and there she was, standing naked in front of me. She was grinding my cock and balls with her hands. I immediately kiss caressed and gave each rib of her desirably edible E trains exterior a tongue washing molesting massage.

After what you might call foreplay for the next event being birthed from the afterglow of our last performance to keep our senses satisfied. We were ready to compare the comforts of her queen-size bed to that of the laid down seats in the driver education car. Sabrina had turned her tonsil-ized tunnel of love into a wide-open mouth, ball swallowing slider-ride. She was performing unbelievable self-satisfying, cum swallowing slider-rides. I could not stop cuming if I tried. She had placed an open season on my cum container and just kept sucking. Treasuring the trail of temptation for the test-taste of armpits and titty nipples sweet sweat, I began a mouth molestation, soft lip roll, and tongue twirling trip across the top of Sabrina's torso. I started with her right armpit and blazed a mouth, tongue, and lip, molesting trail of torment. The remnants of such fell mostly on my shaft, as it discharged another mother load and gave Sabrina the opportunity to lick her plate clean once again. Favoring each titty with the devouring intentions by nipple nipping. Then to the salivating sweet-sweat tongue surfing climax of her left armpit. Staying true to the desires of my tongue, trailing down her rib cage and across the top of her tummy. Then performed a sensual flavored tongue fucking to her bellybutton. I continued to tantalize her twat of temptation with titillating torture from my talented tongue. When I was satisfied that Sabrina would permit permanent pussy pleasuring presence, I laid claim to my final resting place. Sabrina's glorious clitoris, and I kissed her pussy lips. Without question we eventually resumed our love connections desires for what was to become our favorite position.

We had partaken of a satisfyingly sexual full course love meal by means of the **"Ole" Taurus Trait, ("69"er).** For the second time in the same night, in different atmospheric settings of course, and without total body consumption. We began to explore other avenues of sexual satisfaction by venturing off into another world that included the position of missionaries. Although it was not our position of choice it did not take long at all for my cock and balls to feel right at home stretching the walls of Sabrina's pussy parlor. She started showing signs that made me feel as though my prick was a necessary commodity for its vaginal cavity plugging performances and E Train travels. Sabrina found so many different ways to let me know she appreciated every orgasm her body blessed her with. It was obvious the properties of her pussy had not been pleasured by the presence of a prick as much as she would have liked. Every time I would lift up on her ass and drive my shaft deep into her vaginal canal or perform the deep ream stretching process of her pussy walls or bring her to a bliss filled mini blast of orgasmic explosions by cock crushing her clit. Sabrina would respond by tremble-tearing with a screaming cry and kiss me. Then tell me that had never happened before. She would scream, "Oh, it feels good, do it more and more, go in deep, go in deep." When I pulled my cock out of her, so obviously, deprived pussy to pursue and pleasure another one of her treasures, Sabrina pushed her pussy up on my shaft so she would be able to stay in touch with my prick as it departed. She tried hard to preserve our body's connection as she cried and screamed, "No, no, please stay, do more." Then I slid my lubricated jewels up between her tits and started titty fucking her. The same thing happened when I lifted her arm and lubricated her armpit. She went nuts. Sabrina responded like most virgins do. But I knew that was not possible. She had a daughter named Sonja that was 14 years old.

    I just kind of let all that be as it may. I let her cry and kiss, scratch, and squeeze me with all her might in repayment for the pleasures I was providing for her. I felt good about just performing as long as she wanted me to in any way she wanted, and that is exactly what I did. I worked my ass off and did everything I could think of just to hear her cry and scream for more. I even pulled my cock out and started jacking off on her breast. Sabrina grabbed my cock with both hands and helped me. When my shot went off, I think it fell on the other side of the room.

Sabrina's reward for her part in that performance was only a few dribbling drools that landed on her titties. We massaged them gently with our hands and my cock and nut sack. Then we did a repeat performance of the triple handed Jack off process for her pleasure. We even returned to the ("69"er) for another satisfying half hour to 45 minutes of consuming each other's love potion from clit and cock orgasmic bliss explosions. She jerked me off and pointed my prick so the cum would land all on her face. Then rubbed it through her hair. There was nothing Sabrina did not want to try over and over again.

To help Sabrina build her knowledge and desires for a pleasurable love making foundation, I returned to the missionary position several times. One time I totally knocked her socks off and fucked her senseless. I turned her body almost totally onto her right side and lifted her left leg over my right shoulder. Then I gifted her with a performance of rapid-fire pussy plunging. I emptied my cum container into her pussy parlor's reception room just as my motor stalled. Sabrina was crying and screaming, "More-more-more-oh-no I want more!!!" I collapsed on her body where we locked our lips with a lingering kiss of love and slobbering suction that guaranteed total two tongue extraction if continued. The young lady who taught me how to use this body and leg maneuver, told me it would provide better leverage and deeper penetration. That young lady was absolutely correct, and a great lovemaking machine, as Sabrina would also become. I can still feel her and Sabrina's fingernails digging into my back and pinching my ass when I look at their pictures on the walls of my wonderful world of afterglow. The only sexual avenues we did not pursue was the puncturing of the prune. And that is because I never liked to subject my partners to that particular act of sex. That would usually have to be their choice, it certainly was not mine.

We enjoyed many more extremely satisfying adventures through the personalized process of driver education and lovemaking classes. Sabrina held true to her commitment of keeping me around a lot longer than I thought she needed to. When I informed her that in my opinion, she did not need any more driving lessons. She responded by saying, "I think since I already have a license, I should be the one to make that decision." Later that night I asked, "When would you like to have your next lesson my dear? She replied, "Pat, I want you to be the instructor that teaches my daughter." I came back with, Sabrina, honey that is two years from now. By that time, you will be a better driver and a better lover than I am. Why don't you just call me when Sonja turns 15 and eight months?" She said with a smile. "I hope you are right about me being better than you in both ways, but I doubt it. I do not know much about how you drive but I like the way you make love. You will always be better than me at lovemaking. I wish you, or someone like you would have been my first. Now to answer your question, I would like to set up a driving lesson every Tuesday and Thursday night at 930 for the next six months. I would also like for you to come to dinner once a month. You may pick the day as long as Sonja is home from school. I want her to get to know you better so when it is time for you to teach her, she will feel more comfortable being with you. Now you know how serious I am about keeping you around as long as I need to." I looked at her and took her in my arms. Then I gifted her with a kiss that held no tongue extraction or sexual intentions. It was a rather long soft tender kiss of love and appreciation. We both looked at each other with watery eyes and I said, "You know, you are the boss. Whatever you want is what we shall do. How about we start the dinner engagements for Sonja this Sunday?" She replied, "That would be nice, we usually have dinner around six.

Sabrina and I had a serious conversation about getting to know things we had not discussed before. She told me her first sexual experience was not the way it should have been. To make a long story short, she had been raped by one of her neighbors and he was Sonja's father. That is why they came to this country and Sonja attended a private girl's school. Sabrina was trying to protect her as much as she possibly could without causing a problem between mother and daughter. She was hoping to prevent Sonja from experiencing the unpleasantries life had bestowed upon her. She told me that was just one of the reasons she wanted to make sure I was the one that taught her to drive.

Sabrina also told me the way her first sexual experience took place, and having a child, made her not want to have sex ever again. She very plainly said to me, "You almost got a virgin when we first got together. You are the first one I have actually performed sexual intercourse with since that time." She went farther and said, "I have kissed a few people and given a few blow jobs. My first few times with you probably made you wonder why I was acting like I did. All the things I am telling you now are the reasons I want to keep you around as long as I need to, and especially for Sonja's sake. I thank you very much for understanding and wanting to help me protect her."

I started to say goodbye and that I would see her on her next appointment, but in her eyes was that certain look of love and afterglow to insist I do otherwise. I looked at my watch and then glanced back to her and asked. "Do you have plenty your favorite wine?" She nodded her head yes. I said, "Great, I have several toasts I would like to make to you, if you don't mind." Sabrina gave me that certain smile and said, "That is fine, I would like for you to make toasts." She brought out a new bottle of wine and set it on the table. I said to her, "You relax, and let your mind be free so it can catch up with your body later. I need a couple minutes to prepare things in your bedroom. Just get a couple glasses and bring the bottle and your beautiful body to bed when you are ready to be totally toasted. It will not take me long to make preparations for you.

I took a few things and went into the bedroom to prepare the bed for her body and my toasts. When she walked in, she had a look of surprise on her face and asked, "What are you doing?" I replied, "I have prepared a special place for a special lady to lay comfortably as I empty this bottle making a total body toast to her scrumptiousness. I have never tried this before. I have this overwhelming desire to do something special and different for you. You gave me that overwhelming desire Sabrina because you are different and incredibly special. I hope this toast will let you know just how special you are to me, and not just a waste of good bottle of wine. I am presently being informed by your favorite lollipop, just how heavy my desire to mouthingly molest every fraction of an inch of your gorgeously voluptuous body is weighing on its mind. It is crying for your touch my dear." Sabrina immediately paid special attention to my love-stick lollipop and solved its problem. I continued with, "If you would be so kind as to pour us each a glass of wine, we can make a pre-toast to the happiness and fun we bring each other." We made a rather lengthy and very personal pre-toast that brought the taste of tender tears and several blissful blasts of cum to us both. It also secured Sabrina's status in my **"Wonderful World of Afterglow"**. She proposed a toast to the head of my cock and preformed a long quadruple wine saturated rim role. My cum container blew a gasket and flooded her esophagus. She slobbered through a gobble-choke on the wine and cum, then started crying and jerked my cock faster while trying to say more-more with her mouth filled with wine, cum, and cock, muffled slightly with her German accent.

After we had finished our pre-toast for happiness, I helped Sabrina stretch out her arms and legs. Forming her body into a total spread-eagle display in the middle of the bed. Then I said to her, "You may respond in any manner you wish, my dear. If you want another drink all you have to do is ask. It is my intentions to ravish every inch of your beautiful body with your favorite wine covering. I will apply it with my mouth lips and tongue, yes, and even sometimes my love-stick. I shall try to spill as little as possible. When I do spill, I will track it down and retrieve it with my tongue." She looked at me and took one hand and started rubbing my cock. With the other hand she toyed with her clitoris and pussy lips, while sensually rubbing her tongue over her lips and nibble nipping them with her teeth. **Holding up the bottle, I said, "Sabrina,**

my gorgeous little German lovemaking machine. I would like to propose a total bottle body toast to your very beautiful and totally edible body. Your scrumptiously overpowering ways, of displaying the wonders of woman". And I began Sabrina's toasted body, wine massage.

I never missed a spot from her hairline to the tip of her toes, both front and back. I tongue washed with wine the entirety of her face, ears, and the nape of her neck. Administering an individual rib tongue travel for the exterior of her E train/(esophagus). Salivating and slobbering with wine saturation of her armpits, and tongue tracking her arms to her fingertips with individual finger sucking. I performed a sensual lick-lip trace-kissing to the palm of her hands. Crisscrossing Sabrina's upper to middle torso provided me the pleasures of total saturation to her breasts with satisfyingly sexy nipple sucking. Doubling back from time to time for the sweet sweaty taste of two tits with wine. I took her bellybutton by surprise with an open mouth tongue diving splash. I filled it again and again, each time carrying it back share with Sabrina. She was smiling with kind of a whimper weep. I asked her what was wrong. She told me she did not have anything to play with. I said "Appreciate your body, you have an extremely beautiful and voluptuous one. Give your titty's a tender touch and spread your Palace door for finger fucking from time to time. I will make my body parts available to you sooner than you might think." As I tongue and mouth traveled her middle torso, I circled her pussy two or three times then traveled on down the legs to her toes. I tenderly applied a toe and foot lip-tongue wine massage and blazed the ball of her foot with a suction kiss tongue tickle. Then traced another trail back up the same leg to her twat where once again I circled while dropping several driblets of wine on the protective patch of pubic hair. Then traveled the other leg and supplied the same treatment to it. Then I eagerly lip and tongued my way back to nestle in the comforts of her love nest. After providing myself and Sabrina with a fast moment or two of pussy pleasuring, I put one hand under her butt and lifted enough to make her pussy entrance level. This allowed me to pour a small amount of wine between the lips of my favorite bodily orifice, which I tongue-suck retrieved and carried back to Sabrina's wanting lips. I asked her to turn over on her tummy and told her it was time for me to tongue surf her backside. I enthusiastically said as I mimicked her a kiss. "I shall return to your pussy pleasuring shortly my dear." Sabrina's back was not blessed with as many pleasuring parts as her front. To add excitement for both of us on my trip of tongue surfing her back I pleasured her pussy and clitoris with finger fucking action. Body surfing her back with my tongue was a rather interesting little trip but did not take that long. I by-passed her butt and went down her legs to her ankle where I had left off from the front side. I would speed up my finger fucking procedure from time to time to keep Sabrina supplied with little mini blasts of pleasurable clitoral explosions. Once I had completed my tongue traveling the calves and hips of her legs, I took a special moment for viewing her beautifully bubbling buttocks. Sabrina's ass cheeks were perfectly proportioned and came with a recorded invitation that said, **"Please take your time, and do me the honors of soft-slapping, kiss-biting, and tongue-traveling. However, one must be careful, these mounds have a cave. As inviting as it may appear, please try not to disturb the entrance. You may gently tease, with a wine saturated dancing tongue tap, to its door of temptation. We hope the three of us enjoy the choices you make."** I have never been an ass man, but Sabrina's butt was just simply, **too pretty.** It was definitely talking to me. Her beautiful bubbling butt was mesmerizing my thought process by mental molestation. This is one area of the back I wanted to play with. I nibble nipped and teeth pinched, tongue surfed and soft bit, then slapped several times while performing a bouncing bubble butt drumroll. Acknowledging sadness with a slightly deeper sliding bite of departure as I entered her ass crack with a very well lubricated tongue and lips, along with a mouth full of wine. I tongue favored the crevice of Sabrina's ass with flavor and circled the exterior rim of her prune a couple times. Pressing lightly with my tongue I bouncingly-tapped her anal opening several times. Returning to my senses, I tonguing-ly kiss-played with her buttocks and gave them a force-filled hand-print goodbye, then I said. "Sabrina my dear, your beautiful bubbling butt processes so much magnetism, I barely had the strength to depart. Now, could I persuade you to return once again to your eagle spread position of pleasure on the bed so that I might perform a tongue tango with your glorious clitoris."

This was a long overdue move. My mouth went from Sabrina's ass-hole to her pussy without moving my body much at all. Now it was time for us to mix and partake of the flavors of her sweet sweat and love juices with wine. And for the next 30 to 45 minutes that is exactly what we did. I lifted her butt up even higher than I had before. Sabrina saw what I was doing and joined the pleasure-seeking by spreading her pussy lips with her fingers so I could pour more wine in and lip-lickingly-suck more out to share with her. After two or three times of this dual performance of prepping her vaginal cavity to be a receptacle of wine, we were in sync. Together Sabrina and I reveled in the flavors provided by the pleasures of her pussy juices mixed with her favorite wine. Sabrina grabbed my shaft and started pulling. She was trying to inspire the partaking of our favorite position. Obviously, that was not going to be a problem for me. I was a great admirer of the Taurus addiction and believed it to be the ultimate act of sex in the art of making love. It provides the possibilities of two lovers becoming one, much more so than any other act of the aforementioned art.

Since I had succeeded in utilizing most of the wine previously while partaking of the pleasures and fruits of Sabrina's voluptuousness, I could get right down to the nitty-gritty. This of course, was satisfying the hunger in both our minds and bodies for sexual desires.

Sabrina wanted me to pour some of what was left of the wine in her glass so she could endeavor to inebriate the senses of my love package and make them more flavorful. We both took an interest in saturating one another's sexual pleasuring parts. Sabrina took a drink held it in her mouth and somehow opened the entrance to her E train. Allowing me the pleasures of a soft smooth wet rib cage slide through her esophagus as I filled her throat with my cock. I was busy fulfilling my desire to totally saturate her fuzz patch snatch and clitoris and perform my animal instinct lick-sucking process, pubic hair included, until the flavoring was diluted. Then replenish and this time fill her pussy chamber. For some reason Sabrina had allowed me the topside. I think maybe it was because she had in mind doing what she was doing with my slippery slide of her E train ride. It would have been difficult and maybe even impossible if she were on top. After a few minutes Sabrina indicated, she would like to have the topside, and so it was. I was totally satisfied with top or bottom as long as our bodies remained one, so we did a body roll for position reversal. The only thing I was concerned about was eliminating the hunger pains for sex. Over the past two hours of high intensity body travel and very few orgasmic blasts of floodgate status. I had been left with bulging balls and a cum container that was about to burst. Sabrina was conscious of that fact also. She was totally into accepting all releases necessary to alleviate the blue-ball-pains caused by pent up love juices. Sabrina was an extremely special cock sucking caretaker. The first time she force-fed my shaft all the way into her esophagus tunnel of love I pleasured her throat with two ball busters that left her with the gagging gobbles of wine and spillage. Sabrina went after it like a starving animal. With her tongue, lips, and mouth all around my ball and ass crack area. Almost standing on her head in the process. She caused me to release another orgasmic blast just from the pleasure of watching her gobble-chase my lost love lava.

After we both performed and accepted the pleasures, from many different deliveries of love juices, we decided to relax and lay in each other's arms while finger fondling different parts in the calming down process. One thing that interested me was Sabrina taking my hand and lubricated it with her pussy juices. She softly and slowly finger traced her ass crack to her anal orifice. Using my finger, she ream-circled the outer rim several times. Then returned to her pussy for more juices, came back and did more of the same.

Finally bringing my finger to rest on the opening of her prune. Sabrina took one hand and pulled up on her ass cheek, opening the entrance of her prune slightly and very quietly said, "You may push easy." I did and her ass hole eagerly accepted my finger to the first knuckle. Sabrina quickly pulled my finger out and said, "That was my first time Pat. Tonight I give you my prune virginity." As she smiled and kissed me, I said, "You know that is one of the only times you have called me by name, I thank you for the gift, and I am sure you will remember who you gave it to." We said good night and went to sleep.

Chapter 14

Rapturized Ruby

****

THE next day I drove to my office in DC to make my turn in. It was Monday and I purposely made it a short day. I only had four students that day and they were all on the Volkswagen. The other car I used to teach stick shift on. I was scheduled to pick up my first student at 4 PM, and my last one at 9 PM. Working with one-hour appointments I always allowed a few minutes extra for scheduling and conversation. One of my younger students wanted to take lessons on both stick shift and automatic transmission cars. Her name was Mary, and she had already taken two lessons on the automatic transmission car. I purposely scheduled her for my last appointment at 9 PM, to be picked up on the stick shift and then change to the automatic. I had done this before, and she was fine with it. She was a person that wanted to know all you knew about everything and everybody, and she liked to talk a lot. We usually had to stop at a 7-Eleven to get a cup of coffee or soda while we set up her schedule and talked. She was 20 years old, and like just about every other young lady in that area, worked for the government and she loved to party. I had only known her about 30 minutes when she invited me to one of her parties on the weekend prior. My schedule was too busy so I told her I would like a rain check for the next one. She indicated that would be fine, then informed me everyone she invited was about the same age. I guess she thought it would make me feel more comfortable if I knew everyone was around my age.

My first two students were new. My eight o'clock was a very young 55-year-old lady that was the picture of elegance. She looks and acts as though she has been working out all her life, and seems to be in great shape, happy and healthy. Her name is Ruby, and she is incredibly attractive. Who knows, I may talk her into honoring me by serving as one of my training program teachers for the art of making love. I believe someone that looks as good as she does for her age knows a lot more than I do in that arena. I honestly would consider it a privilege to learn from her. The more I think about it the more I like the idea, she always looks good and dresses nice. I will keep it in mind and if the opportunity arrives, I might bring the topic up. Ruby has recently retired and is going to move to the beach and buy a sports car. She needs to learn to drive the stick shift. I told her I loved the beach, and jokingly suggested that I come to the beach to teach her. Traffic would be easier for her to deal with there. She just looked at me without saying anything, but the look she gave me kind of indicated that she might like to put me in her suitcase and take me along for company on the ride. It was five minutes to eight when I pulled into her driveway. Ruby saw me coming in and started out the door to meet me. I had already made up my mind I would not breach that subject tonight. Instead, I would try to find out more about what her line of work has been and what she was going to do when she moved, other than enjoy the beach. I knew if she was going to buy a sports car, she was going to need quite a few more lessons. I figured I would have plenty of time to try to work something out we both could enjoy while she was becoming an expert at driving a stick shift automobile. Quite honestly, I was a little more concerned about trying to get something happening with Mary. I did not think it was a good idea to overload my plate. Especially with lovemaking being something I loved to do, and always tried to give the best performance I possibly could. I was familiar with the old saying, biting off more than you can chew. I knew if I played my cards right, I might be able to appease my appetite for both, but at separate times. I learned that Ruby had been married for five years but had no children. She told me she loved children as long as they belonged to someone else. That was pretty much the way I felt about children as well. She said, "Children are fine, but they require too much time and attention. I am someone who likes to spend my spare time and attention on myself or doing something I like to do. If you have children and want to treat them right, you cannot always do the things you want to do. Consequently, I chose not to remarry and became a real estate agent. Later I went into business with a couple friends of mine. We started a fitness club and sold health food. I recently sold my part of the business to the other two partners, and I am going to enjoy the rest of my life. I shall probably be doing a whole lot of nothing, except maybe laying in the sun and going to a bar every now and then. I am not sure yet, I do know that whatever I do is not going to tie me down. I cannot wait to get my car. I am going to buy a new Corvette." I asked her, "Once all this comes together for you and you learn to drive your Corvette, if I come to the beach to see you will you take me a ride in it?" She immediately gave a right turn signal, pulled over the curb and stopped. She put the car in neutral set the emergency brake, then looked over at me and said, "Honey, if you come to the beach to see me, I promise you that not only will I take you a ride in my new Corvette, but I will make sure you have a place to stay as long as you want to. All you will have to do is bring your bathing suit. Please do not dress the way you are now. The beach is not the place for a three-piece suit or patent leather shoes. It is a place where you wear next to nothing, and sometimes nothing at all. The salt and sand would ruin that perfect leather shine also." I looked at her and smiled then said. "Ruby that is so nice of you. I might hold you to that promise, it is kind of what I have been wanting to happen with you anyway, now your promise keeps the door open." She said, "Pat, I hope you do hold me to it. I have a nice house in Salvo with plenty of room, it is right on the beach close to a bar, and we can have a great time. I have already told everybody what a good instructor you are. When you come down to see me at the beach, I will show you what a good driver you have made of me." I looked at her, then smiled and said, "Thanks, your offer makes me extremely happy, I cannot wait." Then I thought to myself, I wonder if she serious, maybe I should try to work something out for this evening. I thought better about that and asked her, "Where is Salvo, and when are you going to move there?" She replied, "Salvo is in North Carolina on the peninsula below Nags Head, the "Outer Banks". In answer to your second question, I am looking at cars now. I am having a hard time choosing the color, it will be either white, yellow, or red. Then Patrick, my wonderful driving instructor, just as soon as you can bring me to proficiency with full knowledge of driving a stick shift, I will be moving. Oh, by the way, how would you like to go to the dealer with me on our next lesson and maybe go for a test drive?" I replied, "Sure, I would be happy to do so. My only question is whether you are ready for that much power. You do understand course, there is considerable difference between the power of a Volkswagen and the power of the Corvette. And quite honestly, if you don't know how to handle the power you might get yourself into a situation you are unable to deal with." Ruby responded quickly with, "Oh no honey, you would be driving. I just want to sit in it and get used to the idea that soon it will be mine. You must understand, I have been planning this whole thing for a long time. I will probably want to do the same thing maybe three or four more times before I am ready to buy it and drive it away from the showroom myself. I am trying to eliminate as much of the nervousness as possible. The way I feel about it is, the more often I am around the Corvette, the more comfortable I am going to be there, whether I am driving or not." Ruby was excited about retiring, she was excited about moving, and she was really excited about her possible new Corvette. She really had no intentions of stopping the conversation and continuing her driving lesson. I let her keep talking until she gave me a break long enough that I could get in without interrupting her, and then I said. "I agree with you, I think you are using good judgment in the way you are going about purchasing your new car." I was afraid to say Corvette, she seemed like every time that word came out of her mouth, she was having an orgasmic blast. And that was fine too, which gave me an idea. I am going to purchase a small model of a red Corvette and give it to her on her next driving lesson. I do not want it to look like I am partial to red, so maybe I should get a white and yellow one also, no, I am partial to red.

We eventually finished Ruby's lesson and I managed to pick up Mary only 10 minutes late. She was not unhappy, it was not in her basic makeup, or character. Mary seems to have a happy attitude all the time. I let her drive the stick shift for the whole lesson. I told her I would add a little time to a couple of her lessons to make up for the few minutes I was late. She told me that was not necessary everything was fine. I always parked the other car in the back of the Hickory Chick parking lot. I had noticed Dwight's car was still there and some other training car from a different driving school. I parked beside the automatic transmission car that I was going to pick up and let Mary drive home in. Then I told her I needed to go to the restroom, and I was going to go into the Chick for a minute if she did not mind. I told her a friend of mine was there and he probably would want to talk a couple minutes, and I would be pleased if she accompanied me. I explained he was my supervisor. She agreed and got her purse. As we walked to the front door, I attempted to give her a preview of coming attractions so she would not be too surprised about comments made when we entered the restaurants bar area.

The first person I saw when we walked in was Dwight. He always sat at a special larger booth off from the entrance when it was available. There were a couple other instructors sitting with him but no students. Dwight immediately responded when he saw me with, "I wondered where the hell you were, I saw the ambassador out back. I guess I should have known you be out with some gorgeous young lady. Some instructors have all the luck. Set down and grab a pitcher and a couple glasses. I know we need to talk about something I just can't remember what it is." I told him I need to hit the restroom and asked Mary if she wanted to sit down for a minute while I was gone. She was all smiles and replied, "No problem, I have a beer and talk to your friends while you are gone." Dwight smiled and said, "She's thirsty man, get a picture, you'll be back in a minute. Don't be so damn cheap, you spend too much money on clothes. It won't hurt you to spend some on this pretty young lady and your friends. I'll order for you, go on to the bathroom that way you be back sooner." I gave Mary a questioning glance, she said, "It's okay, you said he was your supervisor, I'll be alright, and we have plenty of time."

When I got back to their booth Dwight and Mary were involved in a conversation about driver education. Dwight ended the conversation with, "One thing you should always remember Mary, is how you were taught to handle a situation. And of course, try to drive in a safe manner, the way you were taught. Do everything your instructor tells you to, as long as it is within reason. He smiled and winked at her then said, especially, when it comes to this guy, Parsons." The other two instructors got up and excused themselves. They said they should be going because they had early morning students. I did not catch your names and they never introduced themselves when I returned.

I looked at Mary and said, "I suppose we should be going it is 10:30." Mary immediately said, "I have plenty of time. I don't know about you, but I know you and Dwight need to talk. I will help empty the pitcher while you are talking." Dwight said, "See, I told you she was thirsty." Our conversation did not have anything to do with what Dwight and I needed to talk about. We talked about the Hickory Chick, Mary's work, and why she needed to take lessons on both cars. Dwight asked her, "Which car do you like the best, and which one do you feel the most comfortable in?" Mary replied, I like the automatic because it is nicer, and of course, easier. But I feel more comfortable in the stick shift, I think because it is smaller. The automatic is almost like a luxury car. It has lots of nice features, the seats even lay down." I jumped in with yeah, "You have to watch out for that, if you get too comfortable you might go to sleep while you are driving." Dwight said, "Honey, if all you had to worry about with Parsons as your instructor using a car the seats laid down in to teach you on, you wouldn't have to worry about anything." Mary came back with, "That was one of the first things he made sure I knew how to operate." Dwight said, I can imagine the importance he put on how to adjust your seats properly and safely." Mary said, "Yes, he showed me all the different positions and adjustments. Then he told me I could lay the seats down and if I wanted to and I did. I can see how that could be a fun feature. I do not think it's a necessary feature for a driver training car, but it is a fun one." Mary looked at me with a smile and asked, why do you have a driver training car with the seats that lay down?" As I looked at Dwight for confirmation I replied, "I did not order that car with anything on it, that particular model comes with that feature and the company wanted a Rambler Ambassador. Isn't that right Dwight?" Dwight responded with, I am just a supervisor, I don't know what the company does I just do what they tell me to do. Let's finish this picture it's after 11 o'clock. I got to get home, my wife's going to kill me." As he got up, he was smiling and continued with, "Mary, you're a beautiful young lady. It was a pleasure meeting you. I wish you were my student, oh by the way, be careful with that seat I suppose it can be fun. Parsons, you make sure you get this young lady home safe and teach her to drive. She does not need to know how to lay your seat down. I'm just kidding. You all drive safe, and I will talk to you later." I looked at Mary and smiled and asked, "Do you want something else to drink?" She asked, "Can we have something to go? You do not mind driving, do you? I do not think I should." In those days it was not against the law to have an open container in the car. So, I agreed to get some beer to go and told her I would drive."

I opened the door on the instructor's side for her and she almost fell into the seat. I noticed when I sat down and started the car, she had already laid the seat down and said, "Wow I could go to sleep right here." I said, "Yes, I am sure we both could but that would not get you home, would it. I have heard that sometimes these seats stick, and they will not come back up, so be careful." Mary came back with, "Well then, I guess you would just have to drive me home laying down. Pat lay your seat down and come over here." I laid my seat down rolled over on my right side and she reached up to welcome me into her arms. I realized right away the beer was having a much greater effect on her than it was on me. I gave her a soft sweet non-lip biting, non-tongue suction kiss. Then raised my head up a little and she said, "Somehow, I knew you would be a good kisser. Thanks for the confirmation." I replied, "My dear, you are very welcome, anytime you need a confirmation please let me know. Right now, I believe the best thing I can do is get you home so you can drink another beer. It will be extremely difficult for you to try to drink beer laying down, so set your seat up and we shall head for your house." She said, "I could drink in this position if you were down here with me." I replied, "Mary, I want you to believe me when I say, there is nothing right now I can think of I would rather do than lay here and have a beer with you. We could have a very deep, friendly conversation about the first thing that comes up. However, the Arlington County police officers usually patrol this area and check all the back store parking lots. I think we should probably head on up the road toward your house." She, whining and whimperingly said, "Oh pooh, I guess I have to wait till my next party to find out just what you are like."

When she pulled her seat back into the upright position, I said to her "Mary, we have another lesson on Wednesday at the same time. Would you like me to bring this car? Maybe if you are still interested you could take Thursday off. Then I would have plenty of time to show you what I am like. And you, my dear Mary, would be sober enough to enjoy it and understand what was taking place." She looked at me with a big, inebriated smile and said, "Would you do that for me?" I came back quickly with, "Yes ma'am I sure would, just for you honey." Slurring her words slightly She said, "That would be great Pat, maybe we could have our own little private party." Trying to make sure she understood I was looking forward to our next lesson also, I appeased her desires by saying, "We absolutely can, just the two of us my dear. I am also looking forward to finding out what you are like, and what you like. You must be sure to let me know." Mary came back with the same voice displaying an obvious state of inebriation. She had too much to drink too quickly and said, "But Pat, I thought you knew what I wanted. I want to learn to **d-ri—v-e.**" It seemed Mary was trying to give the word drive a special meaning. She continued with, "I know you know what I like. I am just like you. I like to have as much **f-u-n** as I can." Again, with special emphasis on fun. I made sure she got into her apartment all right and gave her a little kiss peck on the cheek and a pat on the butt and told her to get inside go to sleep. She responded. "I have all this beer to drink, aren't you going to help me." I said, "I need to get some sleep. I have an early-morning student tomorrow, so I will see you on Wednesday evening my dear. You might want to get some rest and save the beer for tomorrow."

The next morning before I went to work, I was going over my schedule and realized that I had 12 new students last week. This meant I would have to change cars more often. After I picked up my first student I stopped and called the office. I explained the situation to them and told them to block my schedule off for new students until the following Wednesday. Since I was doing the rebooking of my students one day at a time, I thought that would give me enough time to organize the changing of cars. They agreed and got the office manager to sign the approval form.

The way I looked at it, I would probably need at least half a day or more on Thursday to recuperate from Mary's, so-called, private party. I was not too worried about organizing the changing of cars. They were always parked in the same place, which made it easy. I was however, slightly concerned about the number of new students and having enough openings to rebook them in a timely manner.

Concerning myself more with students I had scheduled for the present day, I found some satisfaction when I realized Ruby had been rescheduled for this evening. Her appointment was for 8 o'clock and for some reason I had not scheduled anybody after that. I think it may have been because she wanted to go to the car dealer and test drive a Corvette. I also noticed she had four more appointments scheduled every day at the same time except

Saturday and Sunday. This of course, could present a possible problem for her appointment on Thursday evening. I made a checkmark in my book to remind me to discuss a possible problem for that appointment. I wanted to make sure Ruby and I stayed on good terms. I liked the idea of her invitation to the beach and possibly fulfilling my desires to have her as a sex instructor for the art of making love.

My schedule was filled with interesting new students that qualified in almost every way for the expectations I had become accustomed to from this job. My day went by very quickly and before I knew it, I was picking up Ruby. It was a nice calm evening. Ruby was sitting on the steps of her porch when I got to her house. She quickly jumped up and ran to the passenger side of the car. She said, "You drive, I want to go directly to the car dealership before they close. We can take a lesson afterward if you still have the time." I said, "That's fine, I have plenty of time. Nobody is scheduled after you tonight, my time is your time, dear Ruby. Do with it as you wish, as long as it makes you happy." She explained she had called the dealership and spoke to the salesman she had been working with and they would be expecting us.

It was just the two of us on the test drive which made it a little easier for me to communicate with her. I pulled into a 7/11 to get a drink. I looked over at Ruby and was going to ask her if she wanted something to drink. She was sitting there smiling as though she had realized a dream. I said to her. "You look so pretty and content sitting there. You look just like you belong where you are. It makes me happy to see that look on your face my dear." She looked over at me and said, "Thank you, that is very nice of you." Very fast, with the same smile on her face leaned over and put her hands on my face. Ruby pulled us into a short, quick, and hard lip lock then said, "Wow, I enjoyed that more than I thought. Could we try that again?" I responded with, "I have been in bad need of that since we first met. ***Your wish is my command, now for a time I put my heart in your hands;" I reached out to improve on what she had planned, it was proving to be more than she could stand; Ruby*** *flew across the console into my arms, locked lips with mine and once again displayed her charm; now we were no longer strangers in the night, sharing feelings that one feels at loves first sight; We both shared the same taste of tepid tears for her delight, as we locked lips and traveled tongues to make it right; I could feel her muscles go, as she set back to let me know; "this could not be from the heart, our ages are too far apart; 'tis from the happiness at hand, that causes me to lose command; or the sensuality from a kiss, that may present us with remiss: Oh Patrick, Patrick, Patrick, I know for sure that you must see, a love like ours could never be; filled with earmarks of a fantasy, 'twill soon become a memory; we will both share happily, still lying far from true reality:"* Then Ruby looked at me with those smiling tear filled eyes, and said, "What a wonderful world "God" has made. Today I have experienced so much happiness. Including the touch of your lips and the taste of your tongue with the tenderness that comes from being young. And I get to go on a test drive in a Corvette. What else could I ask for? Now let us have a cup of coffee. We can talk about this later." I never said anything, I thought it best to let what she had said sink in before I responded.

We both got a cup of coffee and walked back outside. I stood on the sidewalk in front of the car and watched Ruby as she walked around and around and around the Corvette. With each circle she made, the more lustful her smile became. I knew she was about to have an orgasmic blast and I wanted to be touching her in some way when that occurred. I reached out and grabbed her arm as she passed by me. She turned and looked at me through one hand around my waist we both tried hard not to spill our coffee as her body went into a trembling shake. I knew she had been the recipient of an orgasm caused by happiness.

Which is truly a great experience. I am sure Ruby would agree there is nothing that can compare with an orgasmic blast of true happiness. Once again Ruby looked at me with a smile and watery eyes and said, "Baby, we really need to talk about this. Why don't we drive over to that parking lot, where nobody is, so we can make sure were not going to be interrupted." I replied sure, "That will be fine. Do you want to drive? Ruby shook her head no as we were getting in the car and said, "My whole body is shaking, what in the hell did you do to me. I still feel as though I am in the middle of a satisfyingly sexual activity." I replied, "I only responded to your call. I held you tight in your time of rapture. Happiness can sometimes be uncontrollable. I believe you fell victim to an orgasm of rapture. I would be more than happy to check to make sure if you would like me to." By this time, we had parked on the vacant parking lot. She looked around to see if there was anyone. Ruby was wearing a pair of shorts with the stretch elastic band. As she started sliding her hand between her tummy and shorts toward her prize possession, she looked at me and said, "No, I do not want to touch myself. You have that magic touch, so touch me and find out." I put one hand on the back of her neck, and the other one on her tight little tummy. I brought her mouth to my mouth and began a soft lip biting massage and tongue molesting process. With the hand I had placed on her tummy I started a tender finger walking trip to the point of no return, which was Ruby's pussy lips. My travels had been made easier by her shaved pussy. Apparently, that had become a very popular thing for ladies to be doing in the early 60s. Without any warning Ruby's whole body started quivering. She was squirming around and shaking and screamed, "Oh my "God", what are you doing to me?" I sucked her tongue really hard, and smoothly bit the protrusion point of her upper lip and whispered, "Sit back baby, relax and enjoy it. You have been rapturized to ecstasy with uncontrollable orgasmic bliss. Fill my hand so I might partake of your forbidden fruits." Ruby started crying and shaking, she looked at me and said, "Who are you? This has never happened to me before. "Nobody has ever been able to overwhelm me this way." I brought my hand and fingers up to my mouth and sensually sucked her body fluids off each finger. We entered a sharing process as I locked lips with her. I could tell another blast was about to happen. My hand went immediately to her love nest. I collected her delivery of excrements and returned them to our wanting lips that were rewarded by the tantalizing treasures and scrumptiously satisfying flavors of Ruby's love lava.

We were both caringly influencing each other's emotions through the tender times of repeated pleasures. It had reached the point where neither of us had much control. With open desires of lust filling both our minds, we knew the end was not in sight. We broke from a kiss and Ruby reached over and grabbed my cock and balls. As soon as she touched me, she had another shot of ecstasy filled bliss. She looked up at me and said, "I do not understand, I'm not sure what is going on, I can't make it stop. I replied, "Do not try my dear, let your feelings be free. If I might suggest, let us take the Corvette back and stop by my place for a drink." Ruby looked at me with kind of a blank, I don't know what to do look. I gave her a quick kiss and said, we need to check the seats over to make sure everything is okay. When we get back to the dealership, I will drop you off at the Volkswagen and return the car for you. Do not worry, my dear Ruby, everything will be alright. When we get to my place we can talk or do whatever you like. We could finish your driving lesson if you wish.

When I got back to the Volkswagen and sat down Ruby immediately began massaging my shaft and nut sack. She was holding her pussy with the other hand. I looked at her gave her a quick kiss and asked, "Are you alright?" She looked at me and said, "I cannot make it stop, I must be flooding your seat. I am trying to hold it, you made this happen, how, what did you do to me?" I looked at Ruby and did my best to try to give her a reasonable explanation. I said, "I believe, Ruby, the way everything was coming together you were just overjoyed. You received an orgasm of total happiness. It is what you deserved. It is also what you needed. I wish I could take credit for making this abundantly overwhelming, fantastically fabulous feeling, occupy your gorgeous body. I wish I were the only reason you experienced this uncontrollable explosion of pent-up bodily fluids finally releasing rapturously. However, I was just a pawn, someone you needed with soothing words and tender touches to make your rapture complete. I am so glad I could be there for you Ruby. And just as excited to see your happiness develop and burst, providing you with an unbelievable magnitude of sensually satisfying hormonal pleasures. I am glad you blame me, and I will happily take credit for your orgasmic blasts of sexual bliss. I thank "God", and you Ruby, for allowing me to be the final factor. It was my great personal pleasure to serve you such a measure of treasures. I personally believe it was long overdue and you were very deserving. In my eyes honey, you were so much more than qualified to be the recipient of the fruits of your labors. I cannot imagine how hard you must have worked, and how long you have been looking forward to what is happening to you now.

You need to take a quiet moment and think about the building up process. You sold your business, you retired, you are going to be able to live life the way you want to live it. You are moving to the beach and buying a new Corvette. You got to realize a dream and go for a test drive in the Corvette, and therein lies the final factor to your exploding pussy puzzle pleasures. Namely me, with the tender touch that struck the match and lit the fire that made you want to kiss me. You my dear Ruby, were perfectly primed and ready, and I saw that. I watched your desires build as you circled the Corvette. I knew I had to touch you because I wanted to be a part of what you were about to receive. I thank you so very much for giving me the privilege of having this experience with you."

I parked the car in front of my apartment buildings entrance. We got out and started walking toward my apartment. Ruby seemed a little concerned if anybody might be around to see her. She was walking a little unusual with her hand still in a covering position of her pussy. When we got inside and sat down, I continued the conversation. I was still trying to explain and console her the best I could, and I said, "Some people say happiness is a state of mind. I suppose that is true to some degree. We are all capable of making our own happiness, and you, my dear Ruby, are a perfect example of that today. I love happiness, I think one of the reasons I always do the things I want to do is because I want to be happy. If I am always doing what somebody else wants me to, I am not happy. We talked about this before when you gave reference to the children. The timing of the rapturized ecstatic orgasms of bliss filled delivery was all about you Ruby, and how happy you were. I am happy to have been able to create even the tiniest part of that happiness for you.

Many people have orgasms when they are doing something that makes them happy. They say Hitler used to have an orgasm when he gave a speech. Playing a guitar or piano, if done really well, can bring happiness and happiness can bring orgasms. Please understand my dear, I am not trying to talk you out of anything. I want you to stay in this mood all night and forever for you deserve to be happy Ruby. However, if your moments of wonder when gifted by an orgasmic blast of bliss do not subside slightly, you might find your body growing weaker and getting more tired as time goes by. While I am at the beach helping you do whatever we do. I want you to always be happy baby. If I can make that happen for you in some small way, I too will be happy." Ruby looked at me and asked, "Where is your bedroom?" I thought she misspoke and wanted the restroom, so I asked, "Do you mean the bathroom?" She said, "No Pat, I want you to take me to your bedroom. I have been under your spell all evening and do not feel I have enough strength left in my body to walk. I would like very much Patrick for you to carry me into your bedroom and put me to bed."

I had no idea what Ruby had in mind, nor did I care. She may have felt differently, but in my mind, she was the one in control. If I could keep her in a happiness state of mind by carrying her into my bedroom and putting her in bed, that was exactly what I was going to do. I stood up and bent over, Ruby put one hand around my neck and kept the other one in a calming position covering her pleasure parlor. I picked her up and carried her into my bedroom and placed her on my bed and said, "My lady, your wish is my command!!! What would you like my next move to be? I would like to breathe life back into your beautiful body and keep you in a state of tender, non-carrying happiness.

Whatever you desire is what I will do. If you want me to put you to sleep, I will try to do that. The look on your face is soothing to my mind's eye. It has placed a picture of you in total nudity, which is also pleasurable to the pulse rate." She looked at me and asked, "Could you bring me a towel and just place it on the bed so I can roll over on it." I brought two large towels, two small towels, and two wet washcloths, then placed them separately where they could be easily reached. I spread one of the larger ones out so she could lay on it. Ruby rolled over on the towel and removed her hand from its pleasure place then said to me, "Patrick, I have never known anybody like you. Somehow, I totally trust you, I feel wonderfully comfortable and right at home when you are around. You are in charge from this point on. Whatever you want to do is fine with me. And before we go any farther, I would like to say thank you for everything you tried to explain to me and the way you feel about me. It is too bad there are not more people in this world like you. It appears Patrick, that you are one-of-a-kind. All I have left to say is, I thank you in advance for the continued happiness I know you are about to reward me with." Ruby was still experiencing wetness and laying in her clothes. I knew what I really wanted to do for her. I gave it a short mini-thought and decided to work on what I thought she needed most. As I started to make my move I felt differently and decided I should go back to my original idea. My thoughts were going in every direction. I was caught between my desires and Ruby's needs, or maybe the best term is betwixt and between. Could it be I was caught between what we both might want, and what we both needed.

I knew what I had to do so I tried to make sure Ruby was comfortable. After fluffing her pillow and repositioning her head, I laid a hand towel and washcloth close by so she could reach them if she needed. Then, I slowly removed her shorts that were cum-covered from front to back. The results from so many orgasmic blasts of bliss and the seepage thereof. I pleasured my lips and tongue by kissing the inside seam of Ruby's shorts that led from her vaginal orifice to her anal opening, with a sliding lip suction. That performance brought a smile to Ruby's face and a tear to her eye. Her approval inspired a monumental mouth molestation that began with a very soothing sensual tongue stripping of the sweet sweaty secretions that had saturated her snatch patch surroundings. As I kiss caressed her tummy around her bellybutton, I could feel her muscles tighten. I was not sure what that meant but I did not want to overplay my hand, so I caringly unbuttoned her blouse and found the bountiful blessing of two braless breasts. Surprisingly firm and fit, medium-sized non-sagging tits. The perfect size just a little more than a mouthful. I saw a sparkle in Ruby's eyes when she noticed my admiration for her breasts. I gently kiss-sucked both nipples while administering a tongue licking massage. Then I stretched Ruby's arms above her head and surveyed her armpits with my tongue. I worked my way slowly to the exterior of her esophagus. Nibble nipping each rib of her E train as I tonguingly appreciated her chin and mouth where we locked lips, and both became recipients of yet another blast of orgasmic bliss.

Ruby whimpered a little and scream-cried while almost violently thrusting her prime possession up-down and around. She was craving pussy attention and she wanted it fast. I was not sure if she wanted to fuck or play the number game. I of course knew what I wanted, but since this is our first outing, I chose to save my esophagus travel for later. I immediately slipped to the bottom of the bed and salivatingly swallowed her pussy lips while tongue tipping her clitoris. I lip-sucking-ly stripped her love nest of as much love juices as I could gather and carried them to her mouth to share the pleasures of her treasure. During that process I mounted and filled her tiny little love-hole with my rock-hard cock. The simultaneous connection resulted in Ruby's acceptance of her excrement's and my shaft buried as deep in her pussy parlor as allowed. She showed her appreciation by digging her fingernails into my back and signing her name with a bouncing finger signature. Then Ruby achieved the unexpected by pinching my butt and making an unannounced visit to my asshole with her middle finger. I made an unusual sound of love and sucked her tongue with mini-bites, as I drove my shaft deeper and deeper while stretch-traveling the walls of her pussy parlor with the head of my cock. We continued our hard fast fucking, and mouth to tongue molestation for probably the next 20 to 30 minutes and survived at least four maybe five explosions apiece. The fast hard repeating rifle strokes of making love began to subside. Ruby initiated the slowing down process by softly and tenderly kissing my tongue, lips, chin, and face. Eventually we lay side-by-side while tender finger fondling of body parts. Ruby raised up on one elbow and looked over at me and exclaimed, "Damn you are good!!! Where in the hell did you learn how to do all these things, you are not that old. You are almost still a baby compared to me, I loved it. I have never been treated like this or made love to that way in all my life. You just paid for a month's vacation in Salvo North Carolina. This coming summer make sure your ass is mine for the month of July." I smiled and said, "In answer to your question of where I learned. It is a long story, and I will tell you about it in July. Suffice it to say, once I learned that I had before my birth been a resident of that particular body parts parlor, it has been my goal to return to my old home place someday, somehow. I made it my business to learn everything I could as fast as I could. I am glad you invited me to spend the month of July with you at your beach house in Salvo. Quite honestly, I was going to ask you if I could hire you to be my sex instructor in the art of making love and teach me everything you know." Ruby looked at me kind of puzzled and said, "You may think I know a lot, but you know a hell of a lot more than I do. You are the first man I have been with in 10 years. I kissed and played games a couple times with a lady or two but did not get into that process too far. It just was not my cup of tea. I have only been with, counting you, five different men in my life. Hell man, you almost got a 55-year-old virgin." I looked at her and replied, "Ruby you are fantastic, I am going to look forward to July more than anything I have ever look forward to in my life to this point. Now I just wonder if I could introduce you to one more of the tricks of my trade. My birth sign is Taurus, and the Taurus love sign as you probably know is a ("69 er). You have the perfect size esophagus for a tight E train traveling ride and a tight tiny little pussy. I cannot wait to provide both of us pleasure by partaking of the treasure it possesses as I swallow the lips of your tight tiny little hairless twat with my mouth, and tickle-tap your clitoris with my tongue. Do you have any objections to that part of the art of making love?" She looked at me and smiled and said, "I have no objections whatsoever to any part of what ever art you want to try with me. You are too good to be true Patrick." Ruby gave every part of my person a hard rubbing squeeze. Then she gave me a quick kiss and said, "Now, shall we eat ourselves into ecstasy, or a rapture filled dreamland. Which of the two do you think will be the first to pay us a visit Patrick?" I replied, "They are both so much a part of each other it is hard to say. Although I do not hold Master status in the art of making love, that is my ultimate goal. I am hoping, dear Ruby, that you will be the one to put me over the top so that I might achieve Master status. Answering your question, the best way I know how, it has been my experience that achieving an ecstasy filled orgasmic blast by oral gratification is almost like living a dream. The degree of ecstasy flavored satisfaction received by orgasmic bliss, or having an orgasm, I believe depends totally on the parties involved. How much pleasure do you want me to feel? Would you like to see me go out of my mind, maybe end up in a trance, similar to the one you found yourself in earlier. That being the case you have every lovemaking tool readily available to you by mentally determining that is your desire. You know my desire is to put you right back into that same state of mind you just barely came out of. I want you to live there, honey. I want you to be happy and make a lot of love in your life and especially through the month of July at your beach house with me. Sometimes the feeling of ecstasy can happen from two people that really love being together and making love to each other. They might be doing little more than kissing or holding hands. You, my dear Ruby, have a personality that oozes with ecstasy and sometimes bubbles over into an uncontrollable state of rapture. Therefore, you should have a private room in your house at the beach where ecstasy can live comfortably. You should call your house, the "House of Ecstasy." You should always enjoy an ecstasy filled life." Ruby squeezed-rolled my cock and balls as she blurted out, "Stop it-stop it-stop it, you are doing it again. My cum is free-flowing, I cannot make it stop. You knew this would happen didn't you. Oh Patrick, I just love the way you make love. Come on, let us get this dinner started. Keep it going, keep it going baby, I am hungry for your love stick and I want you to cum in my mouth. I have the strangest desire for you to fuck me in the belly button from the inside by going through my esophagus to get there."

Ruby requested topside and seemed to be in somewhat of a hurry to get the ("69"er) started. She put the head of my cock in her mouth and nibble nipped the rim a few times. Then she force-fed my entire shaft into her esophagus. She pulled my ass down to her and forced her head up to swallow as much of my cock as possible to achieve deeper esophagus travel. I guess she was serious about fucking her bellybutton from the inside, she just kept forcing my prick in farther and farther. I took one look at Ruby's shaven snatch and spread her legs wide open above my head, only to find it remained closed as it stared back at me. It was as though that pretty little split open hole between her legs had been lamenting, laying lonely, filled with the flavors of love. I tenderly tongue massaged the exterior of her pussy lips and spread them slightly which produced a few cum drops. I immediately soft sucked and swallowed the cum droppings as I covered Ruby's entire pussy parlor cavity with my mouth and sent my tongue on a clitoris finding journey. That particular expedition was accomplished faster than fast, with Ruby's help. When I touched my tongue to her clit, she rewarded me with an orgasmic blast of bliss that was sweeter than honey. I wish I could have saved it and mixed it with peanut butter. I like peanut butter and honey mixed. I never tried peanut butter and pussy juice, but I bet it would be good.

We feasted on each other's body parts and fluids for a long time. I do not think I have ever had as much fun devouring the scrumptiousness of a pussy. I know I have never enjoyed the flavor of love more. It could have been because of the hairlessness of her snatch, the tightness of her twat, or Ruby's fun filled personality.

It was kind of like that song. *Could have been the whiskey, might have been the gin, I went back for more so many times, just look at the shape I'm in. I'm drowning in pussy juices and happy as can be. Her pretty little legs go up to her ass and just won't set me free. I feel like I'm on a mission to set her ass on fire, I can't quit now, I'm halfway there and damn sure am not tired.*

I do not think five minutes separated any of Ruby's verbal array of wonder working words. She would, what seemed like try to talk with her mouth full of cock, and the way the words came out, you just knew she was enjoying herself and having fun. Ruby's vocabulary was filled with slobber spits of cock-n-cum rendering I love yous' . Or the gagging chokes of an ecstasy filled esophagus that tried to talk while swallowing the E Train, engineer, and all. I introduced her to the recently added feature of my upside down ("69"er) waltz across Texas. Ruby went crazy with each sway-step. She was laughing, gagging, choking, cum-slobber-swallow-talking. She was trying to stay in time with her upside-down cock swallowing bouncing bubble-butt-boogie. It was one of the most, if not the most fun filled fucking-making love episodes, I have been fortunate enough to be a part of. It was for sure a rapturous time for the both of us!!! We both survived a most unusual, spur of the moment, enjoyably thought of things to do, lovemaking session, and lived to drive another day.

For some strange reason unknown to me, my day flew by extremely fast. Before I knew it, I was picking up Ruby again. It seemed like I just dropped her off. I think it was life trying to get back at me for having so much fun the night before and was going to make it difficult for me because tonight I had Ruby and Mary on my schedule. Oh well, I always have fun on my job. I like teaching driving it is a have fun kind of job.

I opened the door for Ruby, she thanked me got in and sat down. When I got in on the other side and started putting my seatbelt on, Ruby looked at me and asked, "Do you think you really need that. It is not a law and you're only going to be taking it off in a few minutes." I looked at her and smiled and replied, "I always make it a habit to wear my seatbelt as I believe you should do also." I unbuckled it quickly and put it back over my shoulder and said, "See, that only took a couple seconds, and it is a proven fact that the couple seconds like that can save your life. From what I have learned of our ways of ingenuity to invent new and different fun things to do, I feel quite confident that we are going to be able to find a way to do those fun things with our seatbelts on. one of us might have to set on the console or the gear shift, but I feel sure we could work it out." She looked at me and said would you like to try that now in my driveway. One of my neighbors told me today that she noticed a difference in me and asked me if I had found a man. Wouldn't you like to let her know that you are the man I found." I replied, "I would like her to know that I am not only that man you found, but I am also your "boy-toy." The term "boy-toy" for some reason sounds like somebody in demand. And Ruby, you know I like being in demand, when you are in command. So that makes me your "boy toy." Now let's get this lesson underway so I can teach you how to drive that Corvette and meet you in Salvo this summer, maybe I'll wear a speedo for you. A bright red one with a sign on front saying, Ruby's "boy toy." Ruby looked at me with a smile, reached over tried to grab me by the balls and got a surprise. She said, "What the hell happened, what are you wearing?" I explained, "There is nothing to worry about. I had to prepare for you and that means I had to dress accordingly." Ruby's eyes were big, and her mouth was open. She had a smile on her face as she asked, "Come on Patrick, tell me what you did." I replied, "I folded a washcloth and placed it over my package then put on a jockstrap. And my dear Ruby, it is a good thing I did. I have already had two mini-blasts of bliss." Suddenly I heard the garage door opening and Ruby said, "I would like to practice pulling and backing in and out of the garage a couple times. Let us pull in the garage I want to see your package cover." We pulled in the garage, and she shut the garage door. She reached over to unzip my pants and I asked, "Does anybody live here with you?" She replied "No, I live here all by myself. Oh, hurry Patrick, hurry-hurry." I slid a little sideways, unzipped my pants and pulled down the jockstrap then said, "Here you are my dear, for your viewing pleasure I perform." She looked at my cock, it was hard, and she asked, "May I suck?" Ruby gave me no time to answer. She stretched her small skinny frame over the console, and immediately took possession of the head of my cock with her mouth. Then with a somewhat muffled voice resulting from excessive suction to my shaft she requested, "Please Patrick, oh please feel my wetness." I reached over and pushed my hand inside the elastic band on her shorts to touch and torturingly travel her tummy skin. Then I performed a ballet finger walk over the fevered flesh of her lower abdomen and covered her love nest. Not only was Ruby's rapture on display from the wetness of early weeping, my hand and fingers became the recipient of her abundant build-up of happy cum-droppings. I could feel her pussy lips moving. Ruby was working her pussy muscles and releasing a controlled seepage of secretion a few drops at a time. I looked at her and said, "Ruby baby, wow, how do you do that? You not only have a tiny tight and tasty twat, but you also have a very talented one. I have never known anyone that could do that. I bet if you practiced you could spell my name with your pussy lip movement. Maybe we can try to work something like that out this July. It is fun to think about, and you my dear Ruby are so much fun to make love with." She replied, "And you my dear Patrick, are the one that causes it. You give me orgasms just from talking and sometimes I cannot completely stop them, so I learned how to slow them down. I read a few articles in a sex magazine that dealt with similar problems and the utilizing of pussy muscle for control." With my hand and fingers already in position I could not resist her twat of temptation. While Ruby was vacuuming the main vein of my cock, I began a finger rolling masturbation massage on her pussy lips, clitoris, and inner pussy walls. It was not like I was trying to collect more love juices but instead almost like I was acting automatically under the mental mandate of Ruby's mind. I knew she had received at least two or three mouths full of cum, because I had busted two or three nuts during her vein clearing process. Suddenly I got this crazy idea and I asked Ruby, "Are you sure there's nobody here and you are not expecting company?" Still holding on to my cock's head tight with her mouth, she shook her head no while tracing the rim of my prick's head with her teeth. I put my hand on her head and said, "Okay let's get out for a few minutes."

We got out and I immediately opened the trunk, which of course is in the front on Volkswagens. I very quickly retrieved two blankets and a pillow. Ruby was standing there licking her lips and holding her wet little pussy with one hand as she asked me, "Do you always carry blankets and pillows in the trunk of your car?" I told her my uncle had told me to always be prepared, you never know when you might have sleep in your car. I folded up one blanket and placed it on the parking light of the front fender to smooth out the bump it was causing. Then I spread the other blanket up from the fender across to the other side of the trunk, or hood if you prefer. Then I placed a pillow on top of the blanket in the same place the folded blanket was covering the parking light and got a cushion from the backseat of the car. I took Ruby by the hand, even though she did not want to quit playing with her pussy, or holding it, if that's what she was doing. She looked at me with a question mark in both eyes and ask, "What are we doing?" I put my hands around her waist and replied, "Trust me you will like it." As I picked her up, I said, "I am going to place your perfect little plump bubble-butt right here on this pillow. You can lay back and use this cushion if you need it for your elbows or your head while you watch me pull your shorts down to your ankles, like this. And do a spread eagle with your knees, like this. As I partake of the pleasing pleasures and sweet sweaty flavors your pussy favors me with." Just as I started to touch my lips to ruby's prize possession she said "You made it happen again, it is not only what you say or how you say it, but when you say it and where you say it. I do not know if I can handle this." With the wetness of the weeping drippage from her pussy lips all over my mouth I reached up and kissed her on the lips and said, "I know you like it and I know you want it. I also know you can handle it. You are a terrific lady, and you will have everything under control. You just probably have never had anybody eat your pretty little pussy while you were laying in a driver education car that the seats laid down in and parked in the parking lot of a restaurant where you just had dinner. Or, laying lovely and looking lusciously lustful across the trunk of their car, while parked in your garage." She jumped in again and said, "You are doing it more, you are doing it more." I said, "I know, because I want to eat more, more, more of your love, my dear Ruby. Lay-back, relax and enjoy, we still have a driving lesson to do." Ruby laid-back on one elbow and watched me as I lifted her butt up towards my mouth and put my tongue inside her shaven snatch, then teasingly tangled with her clitoris. She responded with mini-blast after mini-blast, while doing the bubble-butt-bounce-boogie with my lips and the pillow covered parking light under her ass.

With the soft touch satisfaction of her pussy controlled secretions, we more than satisfied each other's needs, desires, and expectations for the next 10 or 15 minutes.

While I was straightening my clothes and making sure that no cum-droppings were showing, Ruby busied herself by running into her house and grabbing another pair of shorts. Then performed the light cleaning while putting something in place to catch and keep the remnants of her runaway rapture droppings. I had already placed a towel on her seat just to make sure everything would be okay.

When we started her driving lesson, I stopped at the first pay phone to call Mary. I told her I was running very late, and it would probably be close 10 o'clock by the time I arrived. She told me that would be all right and thanked me for calling.

As we finished Ruby's lesson and pulled into her driveway, I said, "We will practice your backing in and out of the garage later. I do not have time for another trunk episode. I really wish I did; I always enjoy your orgasms." She quickly said, "Shut up, you are doing it again." I reached over and patted her on the pussy a couple times and kissed her on the cheek. Then I told her I would see her on our next appointment. We said good night and I was on my way to pick up Mary.

Chapter 15

"Wedding Bells"

****

As I pulled into the parking lot of Mary's apartments, I realized I had the wrong car. It was too late to do anything about it, so I picked Mary up started her lesson on the stick shift. Everything had been cleaned up and I removed the towel from the seat so there would be nothing to talk about. Although I enjoyed the lasting memories and remnants of perfume and love fluids from mine and Ruby's earlier encounter, I was hoping they would not be so pronounced I would need to explain, nor did I feel like lying. I always tried to avoid having those problems.

As we walked up to the Volkswagen Mary said, I thought you were going to bring the car the seats laid down in. I explained to her that I had started running late and did not have time to trade before picking her up. I told her we could go by and pick it up now if she liked. However, she needed to learn on both the stick shift and automatic cars, so it did not make any difference unless she just preferred to have that car tonight. Mary asked, "Is it parked at the Hickory Chick?" I indicated yes and she said, "Let's drop by and you can trade cars and we will go in and have a beer, if that is okay. Remember, I have tomorrow off." I replied, "Sure that's okay with me as long as you don't mind people thinking you're messing around with your driving instructor." She said, "Well Pat, you know that's what I want them to think. It is true, I am messing around with you, and I like messing around with you. And I want people to know that, especially your supervisor, I hope he is there. I enjoyed talking to him, he seems like a very protective and nice older gentleman." I replied, "That is right, as far as I know Dwight is all of those things."

By the time we got to the Hickory Chick it was close to 11 o'clock. Dwight's car was not in the parking lot, so I told Mary he was not inside and ask her if she still wanted to go in. With her quick bubbling personality she replied, "Yes, the one thing I have learned by being with you is, we do not need anyone else around to have fun. You have always supplied, and sometimes oversupplied the fields of fun."

Mary let me know she wanted to have fun and was looking for a playmate. We walked into the bar area of the Hickory Chick and got a booth. There were only a couple other people in bar at that time and no one I knew. I ordered a pitcher of beer. Mary and I began our conversation with the possibility of private party for the weekend. I put my two cents worth in with, "The night is still young my dear, and you have tomorrow off. I do not pick my first student up until 6 PM. That gives us plenty of time, so let us get this party started." Mary came back with, "That's fine, after we finish this pitcher let's jump in the car and drive to Ocean City. I took off from work until Monday, we can spend the weekend at the beach." I replied, "Mary, my dear sweet little bouncing bundle of fun filled desires. I have too many students that I would have to move on Friday and Monday. However, we could leave Friday night and come back Sunday night. Then if you like we could make plans for a longer stay at the beach a week or so later. Nobody likes the beach any more than I do. And I know that it would be lots of fun trying to help you keep the sand out of the bathing suit. Will you be wearing a bikini?" She replied, yes, and I am so anxious to where it. I just got my bikini waxing. I will let you check it out later." I said, "Later is a long time to wait my dear. I know it is going to be easy on the eyes and I would like to find out if it is tender to the touch. Why don't we try it now?" She had on a tight miniskirt which did present a slight problem but did not prevent the pleasure of pussy-patting in a booth at the Hickory Chick, which was a first for both of us. Mary rolled her eyes and shrugged her shoulders a couple times and said, "Pat, you are so bad, in such a good way. Let us finish our beer and find a place we can play." I agreed and said, "I know the perfect place. I promise it will put stars in your eyes and love in your heart. It is only about 10 minutes from here on the parkway by the Potomac River. It is kind of like a lovers-loop where people go sometimes just to lay back and enjoy. Some of them even get out and put a blanket down to lay on the ground." She asked, "Do you have any blankets in your car?" I replied, I sure do but we won't need them, we have seats that lay down." Mary quickly inquired, "But Pat, how do I see the stars through the roof of the car?" I replied, "You should not worry about that my dear, that is my job. Trust me you will see plenty of stars, and so will I." Mary saw stars creeping up around my balls from the crack of my ass and bouncing off my cock as I filled her mouth with star-studded flavors of loves juice. I saw stars as they pole vaulted and jumped over the pubic hair hedge like ridges provided by the bikini waxing that surrounded her pussy lips. Mary's pussy lips were sending invitational vibrations and shockwaves from my brain to my balls. They were running random through my body and up the main vein of my cock as I exploded and eagerly replenished her pleasures of love juice swallowing. The stars were as anxious as I was to get over the hedges and swim through the sweet sweat of Mary's soft wet pussy lips that served as the protector of her glorious little clitoris. I became the beneficiary of even more stars as I tenderly tongue touched and tormentingly tapped on the door to her, unusually hard to find, clit. Mary's butt cheeks started to shake and quiver as she sprayed a bubbling stream of obviously fresh secretions of love into her pussy parlor. There I attempted to lick, suck, and swallow all the sticky sweetness of cum her body produced.

After reveling in the adventures of love under the stars by the Potomac, we had a rather quiet journey to my apartment. Mary sat close to me leaning on my shoulder and kept one hand in my crotch. On occasion she would reach up and nibble on my ear or kiss my neck. Neither of us had mentioned anything about the trip to the beach since our earlier discussion.

As I pulled in and parked in the parking lot at my apartment I turned to Mary and asked, "Are you okay with this? I just naturally thought this is what you wanted since you are not working tomorrow." With a big smile and glowing eyes Mary said, "Yes Pat, this is exactly what I was hoping for. I want to make real and sweet love with you, the normal way." I thought I knew what she meant, but since normal to me would be the ("69"er), I pulled her closer to me and gave her a long-lasting tender tongue massaging kiss, then looked at Mary and asked, "Are you talking about the missionary position?" She shook her head yes and we got out and went inside. After we got into my apartment, I put my arms around Mary and held her tight to me for at least a minute, maybe more, without saying anything. Then I asked her if she were hungry or if she wanted a drink? she told me she would like a drink or a beer but did not want anything to eat and said, "I am having hunger pains for your love stick." I fixed us both a Southern comfort. Remembering how she was the last time we were out I mixed her drink a little weaker than mine.

We talked a few minutes and then I smilingly suggested we take a shower and get ready for bed. Mary agreed and asked if she could have another drink to take with her to the shower. Then she asked, "Would you please make it a little stronger? I want to take it with me in the shower and it might have to last a little longer, if that is okay with you." I replied," "Sure that's no problem, you can sit it on the top shelf of the shower wall. The water will not get in it, I do it all the time."

We went into the bedroom and got undressed. I undressed her and she undressed me. I immediately started mouth molesting her breasts and finger rolled her newfound hedges. Mary immediately dropped to her knees and supplied a super strong suction to the head of my love stick and attempted swallowing my entire shaft. I moved over and laid down on the bed and indicated to her with my position for a ("69"er) and told her I had a special trip planned for her. Mary was gobble gagging, and I was hedge hopping. I suddenly stood up grabbed her by the shoulders and pulled her face tight to my groin area. I tried to display my dancing skills by combining moves of a tango and jitterbug as I carried her into the bathroom. I let her down easy, licking her ass cheeks and prune as I turned our bodies toward the floor, and she returned the favor. I told her I would have taken her into the shower that way, but I did not want her to get water up her nose and maybe choke. Mary looked at me and said, "You are crazy-crazy good." I smiled and said, "Thank you!"

I got our drinks and set them on the shower self and told Mary to adjust the shower to the temperature she wanted. She did, and I got a bar of soap and gave her a bar. I went immediately to her hideaway hedge of pussy protection since that was the area I planned to service first. While doing so I experimented with a little butt-crack cleanliness and teasing prune rim reaming with soap suds. She smiled and looked at me funny then did the same thing to me. Except her rim reaming procedure went a little deeper. She applied just enough pressure for slight penetration.

This made me think Mary might be opening her mind for experimental projects. I got the shower spray and rinsed her hedge and pussy area off good. Then I tried to spread her cunt lips wide enough so that I might be able to spray her hot-spot and send her clit into submission so she would favor us with her secretions of cum. However, my attempt to shock-spray her clitoris into action did not have as much effect as I thought it might. She produced a much lighter load of love juices than I was hoping for. They were tongue worthy and tasty, soft, and scattered droppings I quickly collected and moved up to share with a kiss that she eagerly accepted with a smile and thanked me.

We enjoyably hand surfed each other's body parts, orifices, and protrusions, with soap suds, until we knew for sure even our toenails would be clean to the touch of a tongue. Then I hurriedly padded her body semi-dry with a small towel and told her we would finish drying in the bedroom. I took several large and small towels with me and laid two large towels down on the bed and told Mary to lay down I would pad her dry. While I was getting into tongue massaging armpits and all body openings and protrusions, Mary kept wanting to try to do the same. I finally said to her, "My dear naked and gorgeously scrumptious edible hunk of female flesh. Please do not deprive me the privilege and pleasures of prepping such an invitingly lovely and easy on the eyes body for a soon to come very pleasurable sexual activity from the Art of making love. Enjoy yourself, it is all about you baby. My eyes are filled with your beauty. My heart and mind are overwhelmed with your desire to be here with me. Let us take our time and be happy every second of the upcoming event, which is apparently your favorite. I had just finished prepping her pussy with my tongue and fingers to have a soft tender easy entrance for my cock while making love. I was now in the process of tongue washing her middle to upper torso on my way to the loving kisses before entering her wanting pussy parlor. Mary lifted her head a little, then put her hand on my face and said, "Pat, my pussy is so small, and your cock is so big. Is this going to hurt? Oh Pat, please try not to hurt me.

<u>You know this is my first time, don't you?"</u>

???
??

{THE END}
Wedding Bells rang for that gorgeous young lady

On
June the 26th, 1968

In
Washington, DC

www.ingramcontent.com/pod-product-compliance
Lightning Source LLC
LaVergne TN
LVHW040145080526
838202LV00042B/3029